# GIVE DUST A TONGUE

John F. Deane

# Give Dust a Tongue

the columba press

First published in 2015 by
# the columba press
55A Spruce Avenue,
Stillorgan Industrial Park,
Blackrock, Co. Dublin

Front cover portrait of John F. Deane and back cover image,
'Minaun Blue', Achill Island, by Sean Cannon,
The Western Light Art Gallery, Keel, Achill Island, Co. Mayo
www.achill-island.com
Cover design by RedRattleDesign.com
Origination by The Columba Press
Printed by ScandBook AB, Sweden

ISBN 978 1 78218 218 4

Acknowledgements are due to Fr Ronan Drury, editor *The Furrow* where some of these pieces appeared; also to Cliodhna Ni Anluain, of the RTÉ Radio programme, *Sunday Miscellany*, where the miscellany pieces were first produced; and to Christ Agee, editor, *Irish Pages*. Many of the poems have been published in various collections from Carcanet, in Manchester, particularly in *Snow Falling on Chestnut Hill: New and Selected Poems*, 2012.

# Contents

*One*

| | |
|---|---|
| You | 15 |
| The Deckchair | 15 |
| By Jordan Water | 19 |
| Bunnacurry, Boston and the Western Wall | 24 |
| Borders | 30 |
| Miscellany: The Travellers | 31 |
| Grandfather Ted, whose Name was John | 33 |
| Heritage | 37 |
| Monastery and Colony | 38 |
| Nanna | 41 |
| Achill, the Island | 47 |
| Miscellany: The Rhododendron Wood | 53 |
| That Man | 55 |
| Riverdown | 63 |
| That Woman | 65 |
| Miscellany: The Scholar | 80 |

*Two*

| | |
|---|---|
| Down the Long Corridors | 85 |
| Miscellany: Tracks | 99 |

*Three*

| | |
|---|---|
| Novice | 105 |
| Treasure in Heaven | 116 |
| Seminarian, with Raleigh Bike | 126 |
| Seminarian, with Chisel and Saw | 131 |
| Ordinary Possibilities | 139 |

*Four*

| | |
|---|---|
| Winter in Meath | 147 |

*Five*

Poetry Ireland                                           159
The Book of Love                                         171
Forever a Stranger and a Pilgrim: Denise Levertov        177
Miscellany: Muir Woods, California                       181
The Reek                                                 183
Death of a Brother                                       191
Name and Nature: Who do you say that I am?               195
Give Dust a Tongue                                       196
Hopkins: the cosmic Christ                               207

*Six*

According to Lydia                                       219

## Deniall

When my devotions could not pierce
Thy silent eares;
Then was my heart broken, as was my verse;
My breast was full of fears
And disorder:

My bent thoughts, like a brittle bow,
Did flie asunder:
Each took his way; some would to pleasures go,
Some to the warres and thunder
Of alarms.

As good go any where, they say,
As to benumme
Both knees and heart, in crying night and day,
*Come, come, my God, O come,*
But no hearing.

O that thou shouldst give dust a tongue
To crie to thee,
And then not heare it crying! all day long
My heart was in my knee,
But no hearing.

Therefore my soul lay out of sight,
Untun'd, unstrung:
My feeble spirit, unable to look right,
Like a nipt blossome, hung
Discontented.

O cheer and tune my heartlesse breast,
Deferre no time;
That so thy favours granting my request,
They and my minde may chime,
And mend my ryme.

*George Herbert, 1593–1633*

9

Early in the morning he came again to the temple. All the people came to him and he sat down and began to teach them. The scribes and the Pharisees brought a woman who had been caught in adultery; and making her stand before all of them, they said to him, 'Teacher, this woman was caught in the very act of committing adultery. Now in the law Moses commanded us to stone such women. Now what do you say?' They said this to test him, so that they might have some charge to bring against him. Jesus bent down and wrote with his finger in the dust of the ground. When they kept on questioning him, he straightened up and said to them, 'Let anyone among you who is without sin be the first to throw a stone at her.' And once again he bent down and wrote in the dust of the ground.

(NRSV, Jn 8:2–8)

*One*

*You*

I am sea-born, and sea-inclined; islanded
on this earth, dragged each-which-way, and tidal;

senses shifting as the sands shift, my soul
flotsam. Prisoned in time, and you, love,

are eternity, you are the current in my depths,
my promised shore. And when I part from you,

taking my words to dry, sophisticated places, I am
tugged towards you, sweet desperation, this underwater storm.

*The Deckchair*

The boy was sitting, engrossed, in the centre of the lawn, absorbed though
unaware. In the distance the sounds from the ocean were rumour, merely.
The sunshine held his body in a gently warm embrace. Fragrances from
the escallonia hedge were a whispering comfort and only an occasional
car, passing on the road beyond the hedge, shifted his drowsy rapture
into a momentary alertness. Beside him on the grass the dog was lying,
stretched in comfort, occasional twitches of his body, a sometimes tiny
yelp, from his dog-dreaming. It was, perhaps, noon-time, the Angelus
bell from the far-off monastery had echoed faintly its message of an
otherworld and lastingness of which the boy had, as yet, no conception.
In the corner of the garden, a small spiral of midges lifted and dropped
in a slow ballet of self-sufficiency and from the grove came the murmur-
call of wood-dove and the slow, persistent oboe-song of a thrush.

Near him, on the lawn, his mother slept, stretched back on the green-and-white-striped deck-chair, the ground beneath her an ocean stilled, the breeze about her Mediterranean in its warmth and gentleness. Years later, decades, because the moment keeps returning to him at odd and unexpected times in his living, he thinks he can remember that grandmother was there, too, behind them, leaning her body, heavy and slowed by her years, against the yellow-painted wall of the house, by the front door that was wide open to the goodness of the day, her arms folded across her breasts, her eyes open, her body stilled, aware but not watchful, the aura of her old-fashioned love and gentleness offering a certainty of something kindly and unassuming to the day and time.

When suddenly his mother uttered a small cry and sat up on the deckchair, glancing around her in some alarm, startling the boy into an unwelcome degree of awareness. Quickly she stilled her anxiety and smiled towards him and said, 'Somebody has just stepped across my grave,' and she laughed, softly. He did not understand. But he had paid attention.

Later, perhaps much later, the family is together on a day out by the seaside, down at Dookinella, there under the Cathedral cliffs, with the sun shining. There is a breeze that carries a slight edge of sharpness to it. They are seated on the sand, beyond the great roiled barrier of rocks and stones that separates the strand from the sandy marram grass and the sand-dunes of the fields. The boy is doing something in the sand, building or digging holes but has grown conscious again of his mother and grandmother, both of them sitting quietly on a great rug stretched out over the sand. Grandmother is reading something, a paperback novel, perhaps, and mother is sitting upright, hugging herself inside the wind, her arms coiled about her drawn-up knees. He remembers her as sitting outside the fray of family.

Offshore the waves are swelling impetuously as they always do, here where the Atlantic Ocean is baulked by the long line of cliffs riding out at right angles to the beach. The waves break as a line of foam goes racing angularly across the crests, and the long-flowing tide reaches in along the beach. It is still far out from where they are sitting. There is an under-roar to the sounds of the children calling in excitement, a threat that is kept safe but seasoned in the minds of the adults, awareness of undertow, of sudden depths, of swirling, twisting threads of currents invisible to the eyes of a child.

Mother has been reading a murder mystery, something she takes delight in, Agatha Christie perhaps, but something, a voice calling from the distance, a gull shrieking and the shriek echoing from the iron of the cliffs, or a sudden catch of sorrow, perhaps, has made her pause, lay the book down on her lap so she can watch inwards. The beauty and enormity of the Atlantic ocean cannot reach her here; her ganglion of nerves, of bone and flesh and tissue holds a moment out of the impetus as she penetrates, despite herself, the dreadful wall that lifts always against human littleness. The boy senses all of this, without knowing that he knows, for he sees her shudder, her eyes taking on the wild light of sea for a moment, her face hardening like the dark rock of the cliff, until she returns, quickly, and gratefully, to the artificial mystery of the book.

Later still, the boy was sent in with messages; there was a hum from the two-roomed schoolhouse, her fiefdom; without democracy, for its own good. Here she stood, mistress, the word *mother* would not apply. In the small hallway there was a smell of cocoa and damp coats. He had to suffer the embarrassment of girls, their smirks, their implausible and whispered comments. He stood awhile, almost appalled, inside the door, all heads turned towards him where he stood, flushed and awkward. The silence broke into whispers, giggles, like a breeze ruffling across the waters of a harbour as he moved across to the big desk in front of all the smaller, individual desks of the scholars. There were chalk-marks on the blackboard, the whole puzzle being elucidated in one of its smaller parts; and yes, she smiled at him, and at the girls, knowingly, though he kept his eyes from hers, willing to be free of this, at once, and away.

And now, and here, after decades: the school had become, at length, a woodwork shop, become, after failure, an abandoned husk, small dunes of wood-dust, shavings, something banging in the breeze with mild-mannered impatience, and only persistent island winds blowing in from the great spaces of the Atlantic or the confined sea that is Blacksod Bay, come fingering grass and nettle, rust-work – and love, long missed.

Before all that a date: 8 December 1943. The world was stretched feverish under war. There was a fall of snow, they told me, over the heathlands. Feast of the Immaculate Conception. Mary, mother, standing on the oceans of the world, stars about her head, a serpent crushed beneath her feet. Achill. My island. Call me John. After the Evangelist. And Francis, after the poor and love-tossed fool. And call me Mary, for the day that's in it, and for mother, worn after the pain and tearing. There were men wading through an underworld of blood and muck, uncomprehending. I hear the winter storms crying through the pine grove. Mother. Mary. Mother and son. Madonna. A winter child.

And now the man. Arrived, the river Slaney rich-flowing on his left, moving through the rich and fallow fields. I have drawn up, at last, by the graveyard wall, under dripping winter trees. 8 December, decades late. That certain pause, a small silence, the gathering up of coat and umbrella, the pot with its offering, three pink hyacinths. The beautiful woman I have loved and love, Ursula, is with me. The car door closed, startling through the almost stillness of the rain, intrusive ping-song of the automatic lock, then destination, the rising (like a tide) of the recurrent sorrow of the merely human before loss, its unacceptability, its disdain. And after it all, after all this, the years, the distances, the roads and skies and oceans, after the prayers and absences and angers, what can I do but stand in quiet by the grave, her name and his, only a dream sea-breeze touching through the puzzle-trees the way the human soul is threaded through with impossible longings, that soft rain falling. Stand, nothing to say, all said, winter, and grey, hoping my presence may amount to something, to the words I had not spoken, to sorrow, to pleading, with the three pink hyacinths. I step across her grave to lay them by the headstone, offering a presence more eloquent than mine. I take my own love by the hand and together we stand still under the soft whispering of the mists. And I can hear them all, the women, the one with the broken body laid out across her knees, torn now, reviled, the child she bore and birthed in anxiety and sorrow, God's abandonment of him being doubly hers. I can hear the mothers, daughters, sisters … their cries across time and space, joining hers in an ongoing silence that shatters the world across every century, crying against war and killing, against crucifixion, torture, rape, the face of the disappeared, the small and vital things that are a corrosion against the love that seeds amongst women towards their sons.

## By Jordan Water

⊂৪৯

I have wondered why Jesus came to the banks of the river Jordan, to his cousin John, to be baptised. He did not need cleansing in the waters of the Jordan, and he had not sinned. Matthew has John say to him: 'I need to be baptised by you, and do you come to me?' But Jesus answered him, 'Let it be so now; for it is proper for us in this way to fulfil all righteousness.' By which I think he means that through the Incarnation, Jesus, son of God, will enter wholly into humanity and will participate completely in all that humanity loves, does and suffers. Jesus, later on, was to pray: 'that they may all be one as we, Father, are one, I in them and You in me, that they be made perfect in one.' Is it our destiny, then, to share with Jesus, in his being, and to share in communion with one another?

8 December 1943. I was born that day (it was Wednesday, the computer tells me), in Castlebar, County Mayo. I was baptised (and, of course, I don't remember it, nor was I consulted) in St Joseph's Church in Bunnacurry, Achill Island, a few days after I was born. My godmother was my mother's sister, Patricia, who died early the following year from TB, at the age, I think, of twenty-three or twenty-four. In a poem, through the wonderful power that is the imagination allied to the strength of language, I can become a ghost and be present at my baptism, to watch and tell what was going on.

> By stepping down into the poem I can meet with her, dead now
> for as many years as I am living. See her, with the family,
> there in the side aisle, in churchday best,

and there I am, (see me!) days-old boy
scarce dried from the warm waters of the womb.
Listen! it's Father Tiernan, murmuring; and that sudden
brass-and-polished-wood and hollow-echoing sound is the door

banging shut in a draft;
       (and that's me, too, coming in,
making my presence felt at my christening nigh
seventy years ago); it is my Christ-

ening, in white cotton gown, white woollen shawl, and Patricia
       holding me in her arms
while Father Tiernan importantly
says a blessing on the water. She was beautiful,

that much they told me, later
       (and can see it for myself,
now, in the old photographs) a 1940s beauty; godmother, aunt
       too young and lovely
to be crucified by TB.

And me, a baby, ignorant, innocent, unknowing,
where does it all leave me?

I moved to imagine myself back in Achill Island, at my own baptism, because I was, at that moment, with a group of pilgrims from Ireland, spending some days in the Holy Land. It was my first time there and I was relishing it, touching on all those places that had been as familiar to me from early childhood as the ABC: Galilee, Tiberias, The Mountain of the Beatitudes, Jerusalem, Capernaum and, of course, the river Jordan. We had a comfortable hotel, a fine breakfast, and now we had to step down from our plush-seated coach and make our way along the banks of this river. Pilgrims. Going back to somewhere we had been often in our minds, now urged, if we wished, to don white garments again and be immersed in the waters of baptism, an immersion the way, we believed, Jesus had been immersed by John. Somewhere along this river, this very river, the Jordan. Everything was white, as it had been, I imagine, at my baptism all those years ago:

and here I am, by Jordan river, standing in the flow beneath
the whispering eucalyptus.
                                    We, the pilgrims,
have stepped down out of our comfort

to be close to the river's source, by the fern-green sluggish flow
and shallow curve, willing wayfarers
                                    keen to dip ourselves –
white gowns, white sneakers, dozens of us now, holding hands,

up to our breasts in the stream –
Malaysian, Australian, Irish, Greek – immersing all together and
holding:
                                    one – two – three, and up
to hymns and hallelujahs,

shaking Jordan water out of hair and eyes.

I had never seen this before, the enthusiasm, the joy, the great sense of renewal. But for me it was even more than that, it was a communal celebration, people of so many languages, colours, bone-shapes … yet all of them joining hands together and singing their joy and their praises. I began to be aware that this was, in fact, a wonderfully human, worldwide thing, a universal joining together of people in the name of Jesus Christ. When Jesus came up out of the Jordan waters, the Holy Spirit came down upon him in the form of a dove, sign and symbol of God's delight in what was going on. I have no doubt the Spirit descended on little me in my white shawl in the Bunnacurry Church, but I don't remember it, sad to say. Where we, the pilgrims, were, there was no voice from heaven either, no visible Spirit. And yet a white bird flew past us, a white egret, a beautiful bird, kin to our own, humble grey heron, flying low and lovely over the waters. Back to the poem:

An egret, white as a ghost, flies low over the water, upstream,
            making for the lake; on the further bank
the umbels of the hemlock are a white haze, the pilgrims' hymns

are shaded many languages, and the waters flowing down
    carry off
cargoes of sin, and darkness, down to the tideless sea.


A cleansing, then, and a coming together of humanity in the name of Christ. Standing firm in the flow of the waters, the tremor of longing and hope and faith touching our limbs the way the water swirled gently about us, I closed my eyes a moment, in a longing to be filled with truth, with the light and life of Christ. As these ideas struck me, I found myself thinking again of the dead, of all our dead, and of Patricia, my godmother. Are we not in communion, too, with our dead, who have passed from this living community into the community of the blessed? Wasn't it a beginning for me, that baptism in Achill, and wasn't it an end for Patricia, her death? And then I knew that Jesus, rising from the waters of the Jordan, showed us how there is no ending, there is only beginning: there is no death. For we join with Jesus in the life of God.

Now I am back at the waterfont in Bunnacurry, a ghost, watching the moment of my naming.


I sit awhile, bemused; Patricia
speaks my name aloud, John, she says, John,
    the soft grey of her eyes
lit with a gentling light,
the end and the beginning holding hands
in unconscious hope; and I
have been here before, as if to touch the Jordan waters
will bring me close to her, bring her back to me, godmother,
urging the life of Christ.


And it was at this moment that I grew aware, at last, that baptism is not merely a cleansing from sin, not just a sign of becoming a member of a Church, of a living community, but it is the wish to take a real and meaningful part in the universe, in the ongoing development of our world, it is being entered into a society where there are goals to achieve, goals of peace and justice, goals of love. And the poem, like the river, moved on:

It's a question
              of trying to save us
from war, from – let me say the word – from
evil; question of being held by those who love us
over, and into, the water; to place us in the flow with the purer
spirits,

              the nations
designing treaties amongst themselves and with themselves,
uttering that one word mercy meaning
love meaning Jesus the Anointed One immersed
              here at the head of the waters:

and just like stepping down into the flow of the Jordan, I step
down now into the poem, taking with me the spirits
of those present, future, past, the dead, the friends, the foes,

the blessed, the broken, Damascus, Gaza, Belfast,
the Sandy Hook elementary school in Connecticut,
              the crossroads, bullets, bombs,
taking them all in my arms, here, within the poem, within the
flow of the Jordan,
and praying – please, still it may be possible – still.

Sometimes the great glory of our faith can overwhelm us with a hope that
is wonderful, and that is strong and firmly based. And the poem goes
back to Achill, and back to the creation of the world, and forward into
eternity, into the great glory of Christ.

And then, and now, Patricia kisses me, a kiss
              soft as a touch out of Genesis,
there by the brown marble base, the white marble font
              in Bunnacurry church,
the water poured, and here, by the river's flow

she says my name, aloud: John, she says, John
              and I close, quietly, the chapel door
and take my place once more, here, ageing, and still
a pilgrim, in prayer by Jordan shore.

## Bunnacurry, Boston and the Western Wall

A small, two-roomed school, one hundred yards down the laneway towards the monastery, in off the main road. The rhododendron bushes dense, with the glisten of raindrops at times, and with an explosion of large and pink-soft blossoms. Halfway down the lane, turn in through the small green-iron gate, and there's the school, where I so often, mornings, heard my name called out, heard my own answering call, *anseo*, present, here I am, for here I came to learn what it all was about, the world, the flesh, and God. And all those friends, young and easy, too, at the small green gate of life, Paddy, *anseo*, Seamus, Thady, Seán – for this was a school run by the Franciscan brothers, boys only, the girls' school a quarter mile up the road, mother a teacher there – *anseo, anseo, anseo*.

I am walking home, the afternoon soft and warm, the schoolbag sitting easily on my back. Third or fourth class, for I had already developed a certain boldness and nonchalance as if I had mastered a great deal of what there is to know about this puzzling earth on which we live. I was excited, for in amongst the second-hand readers, the book of tables, the catechism, there was a new and a great treasure, a tiny lead cannon-gun on tiny wheels that would shoot real matches, propelled by a tiny spring, to a distance of almost two feet. I had swapped my new fountain pen for it, and was in a rush home to show it off. And there was Stokes, near neighbour, in his shirt-sleeves, labouring on the road, shoveling stones into a hole, then back out of the hole and into another hole, for that's what his labouring appeared to be. On his head he wore a white handkerchief, its corners knotted so that it fitted his skull and saved him from the worst effects of a weak sunshine. The thick grey hairs of his chest peered from his open shirt, like feathers, the muscles of his arms thrust out powerfully under the heavily-stained, rolled-up sleeves. He stopped, fitted his big hands on the handle of the shovel, leaned on it and watched me as I approached.

'Well, well, well,' he said, in a mocking tone of voice, 'here's the scholar, his head a-burstin' with knowledge an' I bet a shillin' to a farthin' ye cannot tell me what's the Irish word for tar.'

I hesitated. 'I haven't got that far in the book yet, John Joe,' I replied at last, then passed along, preserving a dignified silence, my scholarly eyes diverted. But I heard the loud chuckling that followed me all the way home. Stokes, slow-moving, heavy-soldered, John Joe Stokes, one for the dimness of the snug and the darkness of the pint, one whose life I could not fathom, nor whose longings I could never gauge.

God, on our island, insinuated himself, like the thousand varieties of rain, everywhere. He came thudding down on our bent backs as we hummed our lessons from catechism and Bible history. He was associated with a memory of a bitter people, herded onto piers to leave the safety of these shores for impossible places: Faith of our fathers, mother sang, in spite of dungeon, fire, and sword.

> With a stump of white chalk,
> a squared-off piece of black slate,
> I inscribed, to perfection, the word
> GOD. I remember concentration, teeth
> irritating against the lips, harsh
> scraping sounds as I worked. Remember, too,
> no words of praise or acclamation but only
> small clouds of dust rising as I erased.

There was a big coloured chart on the schoolroom wall, with pictures of bellows, anvil, rasp; I had to tell the process through, in Irish; the horse coming to the forge, the darkness within, the fire, the hiss of water: *boilg, inneoin, raspa*. I had to tell of harness, cartwheel, tongs. There were boys to whom all this was familiar, almost everyday business. But to me it was strange and distant, pushing the language of my country into unknown territory, for we had a brand new baby Ford garaged in what had been the stable.

History was a book against the English, how they pounded, and hammered, and shaped, how they stole our language and undid our souls. The Bible stories were of oppression and escape, of a vengeful God and a slaughtering Power.

(God, we were told, had surrounded us for centuries with his love; why, then, did our hearts so rarely beat high with joy? The famine bodies had filed in silence to the altar-rocks, the people had been true to him till death; and we were taught to revere them, the fathers, those knuckle-breasted lovers of bitterness who had not yet ascended from the catacombs. What wonder then, that we should turn to lesser gods who have not, nor will not, love us with such gravity, such devotion.)

Br Sebastian, should we falter, curved his rod cut from the rhododendron hedge into a horse-shoe shape: begin, he'd call, *boilg, inneoin, raspa*.

I came back, eldering gentleman, having put into the world several books of poems attempting to state that I had, at last, become some sort of a scholar. The monastery school was little more than a tumble of naked walls, without roof or window or door, open to the skies, weeds and grasses for floor. Now the island winds were the masters, moving through the empty spaces with authority. Thistle-dust instead of chalk-dust was blowing through the air. The only lesson left to be learned is the lesson of time, with its corollaries. In my mind, as I stood listening to the sing-song call of a thrush from the slatternly rhododendron bushes that were left, I offered roll-call: morning-time, we small boys settling, and I hear my name called out, hear my own answering call, *anseo*, present, here I am, but that call was yesterday's call and yesterday was over half a century ago. That child, that scholar, that acolyte to a stern God, that innocent, is absent now, *as láthair*, flown. I speak aloud, into the wind, to the dead in their ordered rows, their scratched-upon and ink-stained desks, Seamus, I say, Thady, Seán, I call, here I am, still willing, still learning, still studying what it is to be a human with human longings and a straining towards the Divine. And it is only the breeze that answers, only the cries of curlews echoing from the distant shore.

Two rooms, the 'small' room, for the smaller boys, from lower infants up to first class; the 'big' room for the big boys (and oh the pride of that, the glory) from second to sixth. In the big room we were truly scholars, we were going to get it all straight, from arithmetic to geography to the histories of God's heroes and his militias. Between the two rooms a high, wooden partition that could be concertinaed back, but which rarely was, for what had the bigger boys to do with the smaller ones? Behind the school, by the bushes, the lavatories, dale boards half-hung, skreeks from the rusting hinges. In the big classroom a coloured, mesmerising chart of stars and moons, the plotted laneways of their elliptical voyages; there were pastel-coloured maps, too, of the known world, and a larger one of Ireland, with its counties and its sorry history offered up in cartoons of the great and wicked. In the small room, the words that Mrs Kilbane chalked up on the blackboard, words to be copied down into a headline copybook, were puzzling at first, though we could write our names in melted tar on the roadside walls. The clumpy sticks of crayons, the thin pencils, were, at first, more cumbersome than shovels in our hands but by the time we sat scared before the looming figure, in brown habit, of Br Sebastian, we were skilled at spelling and we could use a pen with a split nib and ink from the tiny well at the top of the desk. Words our medium and our method, our praying and complaining, and words our way around the screeching games we played out on the lumpy field in the early afternoon.

The scholars, their heads a-burstin' with knowledge: I found them, when I stepped into the Burns Library at Boston College, bearing the burden of the title: 'visiting scholar'. Oh I was shy and scared, I, a poor scholar from the two-room school in Bunnacurry, Achill, and here I was, in a great hall of learning, to give a course to freshmen and sophomores, true scholars, in the writing of poetry. I could hear old John Joe Stokes, labouring man, his incredulousness, his mocking chuckles. One may wander from the sources of one's first school lessons, but never forget the real lessons that life teaches. There, in the plush and daunting furnishings of the Irish Room in the Burns Library, I am actually calling names out in a genuine taking of the rolls, strange names, names that betoken the many immigrants from so many lands, Jessica Hincapie, Jay Lin Lang, Heather Bourke Polanczyuck, and all these bright and eager students gazing up at me as if I, scholar from the tiny monastery school of Bunnacurry, Achill Island, can dare to tell them how poetry occurs, how to catch the wonders of this creation in magical words and forms. Tonight I will give a public reading, in what appears to be an Aula Maxima, to an audience of professors, masters, doctors of philosophy and medal-winners, offering them poems on the crumbling of the monastery in Bunnacurry, on the harbour at Cloghmore, on the current at Bullsmouth. I shall stand before them, a-tremble, far from home, trying to hold my scholar's head on high. *Anseo*, I will whisper to myself, *anseo*, here I am, still learning, still ignorant of the Irish word for tar.

Mornings in the two-room school, mornings after rain; a shuffle-off and scuffling to hang wet coats, an abandoning of marvels, our sherbet, our lucky-bags, our marvellous show-off new acquisitions of toys or comics, and then the clattering of desk lids, the slapping of books. I learned, early, the craft of loneliness, though at playtime I ranged and rowdied with the rest and the best of them. I was stopped, often, as I have been always, by harmonies sensed among furze blossoms and the assonant humming of the bees, by the sheer exuberance and near transcendent whiteness of a herring-gull high against the light-blue sky, by the fluttering among the heathers of a swallowtail butterfly, a tortoiseshell, or the hairy crawling of a caterpillar along the steeps of a fern or a lupin stem. I did not yet see the beautiful God in these things, but I found myself stilled by unnameable longing. And then I was back indoors, accepting the rote calling out of rollicking verses, the echoes of the need to share a lunch with one who had forgotten his, or who had little enough to bring tied up in the wrapper of a loaf. It was the music of being, it was the distant whisper of that music, of harmonies certain in their ultimate structuring, a music that was grounded and pure of ego, it was a deep and satisfactory, though not understood, base prelude, the fugue yet to come. And it came, the fugue, slowly, surely, and is swelling still towards its cadenza. For I came, recently, to the Western Wall in Jerusalem and was told that here was the gateway to heaven, here was the great partition that would draw back, concertinaed, to reveal, at last, the glory, the fulfilment, the peace.

> I stand – a continent away
> from the crumbled walls of Bunnacurry two-room school –
> now, at last, by the Western Wall,
> leaning my hands against its massive stones, and seeking words;
>
> 'in Yerushalayim', the Spirit wrote, 'shall be my name forever';
>
> to my left, black coat and pants,
> white shirt and thick grey beard, kippah, prayer shawl,
> a man sways back and forth in prayer –
> *hear, O Yisrael, The Lord our God, the Lord is one* ... Torah, psalms;

our little catechism asked: *does God*

*know all things?* The high partition
between the rooms squealed on its castors, folding open,
when Father Tiernan came
to test our souls; *God knows all things, even*

*our most secret thoughts and actions.* I relished then

the loveliness of the near-rhymes,
the old-fashioned *doth*-and-*dost* of the English, leaving
a softly-furred coating on the soul. I need to know
the rough texture of a wall you could break your life against so

I have come to take possession, of the songs, the psalms,
       the lamentations,

Ruth and Boaz, Jonah,
Daniel in the den of lions – for these are my stories, too,
the prophet Moshe stretching out his hand
over the sea, Yermiyahu's grief before the golden throne

of Babylon, with Markos, Mattityahu, Loukas, Yohanan …

for here is the gate of Heaven, folded open,
where we thrust our words towards the invisible, waiting
      for those
inaudible answers, where we thrust our prayers
into the crevices in the wall,

and speak aloud, *anseo*, look, here I am, oh Elohim, oh Yeshua,
      here I am.

*Borders*

There are borders we cross almost every day without noticing them, moving from one situation to another; then there are borders of enormous consequence, those we cross only once in our lifetime, from the womb into the world, for instance, the immersion of baptism, death ... It is strange how so many of the everyday borders that are still, of course, important in our living, leave little trace, or momentary traces, perhaps, like bootmarks through the slush of snow, like a hosting of small tumuli of ash. There are the steps taken in coming to know the Christ, a step on step behindhand process, disconcerting after so many years that he is still not deeply known.

There is little that is melodramatic to the process, unless you are a Saul metamorphosed into a Paul; it is the reality of everyday living that is the rude intruder into life, it is the everyday real that leaves a smart in the flesh, a smir on the mind. How many days did I pack my schoolbag with coloured pencils, a sandwich of bread and sugar, a 'treat' like an apple or a 'thrupenny' bar of chocolate, and pick my way, scuffing my boots on the ditch edges, down the half mile to school. I was a child moving in a cloud of unthinking, gathering a life out of roadside wonders and the rote learning of verses.

(Though I was not, as I now believe, a child moving in the 'cloud of unknowing', I believe the opposite: a child whose senses are alert and untrammelled, is open the way a saintly contemplative might be open, to the world and its Creator.)

I was a child before the noontime murmured angelus, half-absorbing the lessons of bible tales and catechetical repetitions as I waited for the joy I would always find (though unaware that I was relishing those in-between non-border moments) in gold-furze blossoms spitting open, in the blooding of knees against the bark of trees as I tried to climb ever higher into the breezes, in the absorption over books of adventure in the kitchen corner. Only later did I begin to aim for a steady eye and a firm hand, a holding close to that intruder who pleads for a drink of fresh water at the well in Samaria.

*Miscellany: The Travellers*

Then one day they appeared, the travellers, as if they had sprouted from the earth, and settled on a green patch by the quarry, not more than a quarter of a mile from our house in Bunnacurry, Achill Island. I was excited by their arrival, two great green caravans, rocking slightly as they were drawn along by scraggy horses, but colourful, with crooked aluminium chimneys rising from the rounded roofs. And two carts, drawn by even more straggly horses, or mules, packed with children and a few big, tough-looking men riding on the shafts. We were warned, at once, that they were dangerous – we were not to go near the camp, we were to avoid them on the road, should we meet them, and above all we were not to enter into conversation with any of them. But on the first Monday morning after the arrival, a boy was led into our classroom, 'This is John Joe Connors, he'll be with us for a while,' the Brother said. And at once I wondered: who would be let sit with Connors in the desk? He was put in beside me and for a while, with this fierce-looking, grinning boy, I did not know whether I was lucky or unlucky.

Connors was small, his curly hair in tangles; he smelt of distance, of ditches, pine-needles, of secret entrances to hen-coops; he had pockets full of treasures: a penknife with a nicked blade, a shilling's worth of seeds, oats, he said, but he'd not stay long enough to reap the harvest. Brother was telling the class about Zacchaeus up in a sycamore tree, shifting for a glimpse of Jesus; cherish the small, Brother said, swishing his cane against the coarse brown stuff of his habit; Connors showed me his palms, a horse-hair laid across the flesh, prepared. I usually get to know the master fairly intimately, he said, and laughed, as if he didn't have a care in the wide world. He offered me a small, leaden grey cannon-gun that would fire matches a distance of two feet, and I was taken with it, offering him my big new fountain-pen in exchange.

That evening I sneaked away quietly to view the camp. A lazy smoke drifted from the two caravans; there was a tarped dirt-black tent drawn in under the lifted shafts of a cart; mute and rangey dogs scavenged the borders of the camp and a horse and mule, crestfallen and watching towards unfathomable places, stood braced against the day. Other children, in off-brown smocks were finger-in-mouth and big-eye watchful. At home the adults were telling of stolen hens and eggs, clothing missing off the lines, they spoke of night-time forays, bodies slipping through the dark and making the darkness bleed. Once the big man, dark-clothed, dark-fleshed, came obsequious, cajoling, to our back door; Richard Tauber was singing, from the old Dansette down in the drawing-room: *Lonely on a desert breeze, I may wander where I please, yet I keep on longing, just to rest a while.* The big man was asking to repair tin mugs, kettles, buckets; he eyed me, and I knew a small, inexpressible guilt.

When I showed off my little cannon-gun, Father asked at once where I had got it and when I told him I had given John Joe Connors my fountain-pen in exchange for it, he grew angry and told me I must give back the gun, and retrieve my good and expensive fountain-pen. I was hurt, for myself, and for Connors, but John Joe just shrugged his shoulders, gave me back my pen, showed me some of his other treasures: a beautiful enamel pillbox with what I thought were red berries inside, but they opened their wings and hopped out onto the desk, beautiful, indolent, ladybirds. Then that evening I saw him again, the big-man, traveller, there by my fishing-place against the lake, he was stooped over, and doing something; I was scared of his gruff consonants, his black eyes; I watched, as a fox might watch from the archway of his lair, and when he left I found shore-stones darkened from a fire, burnt-black sticks and up against the bank a midden of eel-heads, eyes open in slime-black skin, teeth bared and pin-sharp; I shivered, with a new sense of horror. When he came again to the back door, returning the soldered tin mugs, the bucket, he seemed to eye me once more, as if I knew too much, and he might grow angry with me.

It may have been less than three weeks later when I walked back after school with John Joe Connors. He told me they were leaving the next morning, and when I asked him why, he just shrugged his shoulders again and said nothing. He told me to come and say goodbye at the camp but I was too scared and I hung back, there at the outermost edge; I watched him climb the wooden steps up onto a small platform before the half-door of a caravan; he turned, grinned at me, and waved. Then he disappeared into the caravan. I felt a great loneliness.

And so they left, the travellers, as if a mist-filled daylight swallowed them; there were small and ash-grey patches clumped across the hill, with rags and timbers and fox-red flitches of things along the thorns; there were ash-smells and cooked-flesh fat-spills, grease-puddles, a fungus-stink of oozed mud; and I found it difficult to hold my place again in the uneasy light they had left behind, a dusk-light that kept on glimmering along once-familiar lanes. And even still I hear Richard Tauber sing: *Lonely on a desert breeze, I may wander where I please, yet I keep on longing, just to rest a while.*

## Grandfather Ted, whose Name was John

Grandfather Ted remains an enigma. Ted. Connors. Though his name was not Ted Connors. His name was John (after him I have been named), John O'Connor. He became Connors because, I believe, he was working as an RIC officer (of the Royal Irish Constabulary) and the name O'Connor was far too Irish for such a job. He was called Ted by us, his grandchildren, because he was a fixer, working at everything from carpentry to farming to anything mechanical, and we wondered at his skill with cart-wheel and donkey-tackle, how he could fix an axle or manage the chains and leathers of harnesses and all such gear. The only mechanic we knew of was a man who ran the new garage at Achill Sound, and his name was Ted Sweeney. John O'Connor, Jack Connors. Ted. Of the Royal Irish Constabulary, intent on the strict rules and regulations of such a life.

I watched him forking daub-like clay into fine soil, stretching twine taut between two sticks so the seeds could go in on a straight path. I can see his nineteenth-century face in a world of sepia order and dominion, once a week winding his eighth-day carriage clock, ticking off the yesterdays. The labours of this earth need time and space for the story's telling, courting haphazard order, for even the stars hurl bits and pieces of their being down on the world and fling them hip-and-hazard out among the galaxies. Ted wished the ageing of all the world to slip into a semblance of consciousness and peace; he lived angrily, with the anger of the forcibly displaced, for history slips past what is meticulous and certain. He knew of wars, the Boer, the first, the second, Korea, and the rising of 1916 lost him his place, his dignity, his Kingdom, humanity striding forward in rank disorder. On a high shelf now, among the books, I keep his clock, stilled for decades, brass-heavy, glass-walled, white-faced like his own in the last days, a little yellowed, a little stubbled:

'reminder of happy and instructive hours spent with C.S.M.I. Connors, from No 3 Squad. 24<sup>th</sup> rifle class, Dollymount 1916. John Connors, R.I.C.'

He represented, for us, the manliness of smoking, the gentlemanly smell of a pipe-smoking man, the calming labour of it, for it demands space, and time, and peace. Ted smoked his pipe. Evenings, after the winding down of his day, came the ritual. On a special shelf of the sideboard, the box of plug, the pipe, the tamper to tamp down the tobacco into the bowl of the pipe, set the long and interesting pipe cleaners to the side, recover the paper spills from the mantelpiece above the fire. Lean in carefully over that open fire and light a spill of paper; touch it to the tamped-down tobacco, inhale, puff, inhale, wave the burning spill back into the fire. Sit, at leisure, and in silence, in the fireside chair, and delve deep into dreams of loss and order, of garden and harvest, of tools neatly arranged in the workshop outside, and planks of timber carefully stacked and waiting. The neat, wooden box of Mick McQuaid plug tobacco was always put back in its place. I was taken by that laughing old man pictured on the box, two great tufts of white hair on either side of his otherwise bald head, a portrait insisting on the joy of his plug, on the sense of well-being it would confer, on the fine taste of the smoker in choosing so well. There was nothing, in those years, of the great and inevitable damage that smoking will cause to the health of the smoker, and the possible damage to the health of those around him. It was Ted's time of self-rescue, of quiet, of satisfaction.

Grandfather Ted sat, at dusk, before the fire; he smoked, gathering silences about him and watching the sudden irritation of the flames when he spat; small tainted drops collected on his chin, his moustache, and his pipe's stem was scored with meditative tooth marks. He rose, at last, to the observances of the lamp, the mantle, paraffin, a globe to warm the darkness, a glow to ripen the corners where the shadows were into myth while every jagged thing seemed to mellow into liquid gold. Then it was time for prayers, the murmured telling of beads among the lingering fragrances of tobacco and benevolent lamp oil. His name rings out, John Connors, ex-RIC, accompanying the grinding sounds of stone and iron as cart-wheels moved on the road outside. Before he died, strange lorries came, carrying creosoted poles; holes were dug in grandfather's fields, posts rooted with difficulty in the blanket peat, men with scimitar-wielding boots climbed up to attach wires that unrolled from spools more massive than cart-wheels. Soon the house was linked, across miles, to the world. Grandfather's own-built wind-charger, a marvel rising high above the pine-trees of the grove, was dismantled, coming down in pieces, and taken away as scrap. The shadows lost all hint of myth, racing like spiders out of sight and the lamp, globe, mantle and paraffin oil, were left aside to gather dust in an outhouse, become antiques, curiosities and, ultimately, collectables. Grandfather sat, at dusk, before the fire; smoking, gathering new and irritable silences about him, keeping watch.

> No photos of grandfather remain
> in the family album; we called him 'sir', he was
>
> stern and patriarchal, just like God. He led
> rosary at bedtime, bead after bead, circling.
>
> I knelt beside him once in chapel,
> proud to be on the men's side, but he kept
>
> nudging me to kneel up straight, stop fidgeting.
> I looked up at the Virgin's face where she stood
>
> niched, hands folded; I glanced to see if her eyes
> moved or if she fidgeted out of her boredom.

Evening, and the red spot on the kitchen wireless was flickering; there were whistling sounds, disturbances, they told me, from winds that blow everywhere across the face of earth. Grandfather leaned in close, one big hand cupped to one big ear. A polished voice came quavering, then fell away, flowed back … something about the Korean War, atrocities, advances, the mounting numbers of the slain. Nothing new, the old man said, and spat expertly on the fire. Outside I could hear the trees scuffling amongst themselves, and I listened to the ever-present seashore dissonance. I pressed my face to the window, there were water-dribbles on the pane, and all the world beyond was worried into breaking patterns. Everything else too quiet; the ticking of the clock, the vaguest humming from grandmother, knitting in her place by the fire; the occasional fall of burning sods and grandfather's sporadic, heavy sigh. I crept upstairs, to the bulked and brass-hasped trunk, kept at the far end of the landing. I opened the heavy lid and laid it back against the wall; beneath the folded, mothballed old sheets and lace cloths of grandmother's keeping, I found the jacket of grandfather's uniform, the peaked cap with the harp and crown insignia. I marched, up-down, down-up, along the landing, I was an RIC cadet, imagined pistols manly on my hip. When I came down again, grandfather was still watching the labouring of the flames, the moist sods shifting as they burned. I watched him, but he was somewhere far from me; with a great sigh he settled back, touching the dark-brown splotches on his wrist.

Soon, he had disappeared upstairs and the house hushed. Now his grave, in the island cemetery, is a riot of neglect, long bramble-vines and grasses taking hold; rushes and meadow-sweet flourish in the wet-daub acres of the field; rain falls along the stones, lichen eats away the histories, the names, the century.

Grandfather's grave
lies amongst rank disorder; a high stone cross
holds the history of the world
carved in pastel-coloured lichens; the graveyard path

hides in weeds and grasses; St Joseph lilies flaunt
white and unkempt surplices; it is creation's
original chaos of delight –
where the old man lies, at peace, like God

before he shook himself out of lethargy
and spoke. *In the beginning* … But at times,
on quiet summer nights, the old man takes a turn
about the yard, tidying away

the empty beer and cider cans, the condoms,
and works a while on polishing his soul
against the final word that will draw
everything back to stillness. The way he used to hone

his workshop tools, because the old man's God
was a carpenter God
whose every word sent some new craftwork out
into the universe

to spin, and swell, and reproduce. You can hear
grandfather make his way back down,
sounds like wood-shavings being swept,
like a workshop door being shut.


*Heritage*

My parents' people
charted their inward sea of peatland,
pegs hammered down, lines taut between them;

they bent, and dug, and saved, while I,
holding the reins, stood on the cart-shafts
legs apart and balancing –

Aeneas setting out, with
yup there yup! to the old ass;
now I explain the process

to my children on the road before me,
drain, bank, scraw, bog-banquet tea;
leave this waste, I tell them,

to lie in peace a thousand years
it will put down roots and, unlike man,
recreate its rich, soft flesh.

A heron stands, still as a shape of bog-oak;
eels have squirmed, like memories, back into the pools.
I turn towards the white-washed villages

and would escape, half-willingly, this wilderness,
shake from my shoulders
my parents' people's weight of faith.

John F. Deane

## Monastery and Colony

The monastery of the Third Order of St Francis is now a – messy but – picturesque ruin situated on Achill Island just a little over half a mile from our old house. It had been established to counter the Protestant 'colony' that had moved into the island during Famine times and that was recruiting souls, Nanna told me, in exchange for soup.

In my memory of it, the statue of St Francis, just inside the chapel door of the monastery, always stood in quietness, in a smooth brown habit with a white corded cincture about his waist, a tonsured head, down-facing eyes, birds roosting on his raised arms, gentle does couched at his feet, and the Devil, bull-shod and horned, glaring from a ring of fire behind him. Sadly, it was this latter figure that dominated my imagination.

In those days we got our milk from the monastery farm and every evening I was sent down with the scoured and shining can to collect the milk. Half a gallon, I expect, is what I collected.

Evenings. Knocked, scared, on the scullery door. There was a yellow light from the chapel windows; figures within moved, ghostly, unshaped and cowled, in some intimate dance with their dark Christ. Within, there was a sour silence smelling of man, of curds, and of wet stone floors. When I turned, after collecting the milk, and the yellow light sent shadows shifting through the orchard trees – their bitter, arthritic limbs, boned fingers, armpits, the writhing creatures of the drowned ark – I knew terror special to a childhood spent in the countryside where ghost stories were told by oil-lamp late into the night. Up on the road there was moonlight, the thump of my own feet on the tarred road, all the irrational rational dread thudding in my soul till the distant house beckoned to me, home, and the music that light makes tuned its strings for me so I could run, certain again of familial warmth, of the oil lamp softening the eyes of Jesus on the kitchen wall.

Why did I never tell of my dread? Why did I not speak it out at home and see if there was a way to remove such suffering from my young life? I think it must have been that I knew my parents would pooh-pooh such fears, that they would tell me to grow up, there were no such things as ghosts, such words: and yet at other times great and quiet glee would be taken from the recounting of ghost and Devil stories in that same kitchen. I think, too, that deep down inside me I also knew that all of my fears were mind-created, that they were no more than projections from my own nightmares, and that one day soon I would grow out of them, I would grow up, I would become an adult, I would send my own children out for milk and tell them not to be so foolish as to fear the darkness, and that the cowled figures of the monastery were God's good servants, kindly men like St Francis of Assisi, spreading nothing but blessing all about them.

With its sheds and orchards the monastery was an island upon an island and in the school I felt that I was white dough in the hands of the monks. In Lent, in Advent, we drove in the warmth of half sleep to early morning Mass; the slow, sedate black Anglia was parked on gravel where yellow light reached from the chapel door. As we moved from car to light, I heard the rooks in the overhanging branches begin to grumble. Inside, plaster saints with plaster lilies in their hands looked down on polished floors. I would watch for the candle flame that one of the monks, Br Angelo, brought up from the cells; the flame grew large and welcoming as I watched it through the cobalt-blue glass of the door leading from chapel to the mysteries of the monastery. The brown coiffed figures on their prie-dieux looked like ranks of worker angels. Away on the road the tankers ferried shark oil – from Purteen harbour where they brought ashore and worked on the carcasses of the basking sharks – to distant destinations where I wondered what they did with the dreadfully smelling stuff.

> Years ago the monastery died. Now
> the roof has fallen through, dangerous beams
> are slimed with bird-shit and underneath
>
> are dried cowpats, sheep-droppings, stale
> odours, dark-green fungi on the crumbling walls;
> there is no way up to the tongueless bell
>
> that waits for the moment of one final clang when it falls.
> I stand a long while, shouldered by sorrow,
> fretting for the words and firm hands
>
> that built the foundations of a faith; the wind
> of the passing of Jesus leaves the air still stirring,
> while softest breathings of the Holy Ghost

rattle the steps of the staircase that reaches yet
towards the sky; here astounding news were spoken
and foreign wines as warm as blood consumed.


You can see the belfry rising still over the trees on that island upon an island. When I visit the ruins, I bring boots, wellies even, the ground being muddy, the rubble manifold. I gaze at the belfry every time I pass across the island of Achill and it brings before my mind and my imagination, very strange and very old notions and pictures. The parlour, for instance, a place I never entered until it had been ruined; but I imagined the monks receiving guests in fine – though small – reception rooms; a few armchairs, a mahogany table, a sideboard; some books on shelves, perhaps, but not many, and all of them devotional, the lives of the saints, Christian doctrine, the rules and regulations of the Catholic faith. Perhaps there was the occasional glass of sherry, no doubt there were bottles of whiskey stored carefully in case of need … and I know there would have been need. The loneliness, the isolation, the paucity of intellectual stimulation. And then I thought of 'the cells' – quiet rooms where loneliness was rampant as dust, where prayers would have been whispered in very private calls; there would have been urgent pleading, where sleep would have been deep and satisfying, at times, and at times broken and harried with unseemly thoughts.

But from outside everything was sacred, quiet, busy. Rooks would have called out of that quietness, cattle would have plodded from the sheds out to boggy pasture; brothers would have cycled out to the shops, others walked to teach in the little school. There were pantry duties, cooking duties, sacristan and bursar and a superior of some sort, keeping it all in shape and in movement. It would have been, for me, symptomatic of a quietly insistent Catholicism, an icon of the rules and regulations that, if followed to the letter, would lead a soul through the valley of tears to the safe haven of a vaguely wonderful heaven, avoiding the dreaded pits of Hell with their fires perpetual, their instruments of torture, and the awful knowledge that pain and all kinds of agony must continue for eternity, without hope of reprieve. I shudder to think of it, even now after a little more than seventy years. I shiver a little as I see that young boy, early mornings every lent and advent, in that strange sense of twilight-at-dawn dimness, of lethargy, the car, sometimes having to be cranked into life, the choke on, the engine racing, and our breaths misting the windows, heading for some strange and vaguely meaningful morning presence in that small and intimate chapel.

## Nanna

⟨⟡⟩

Nora Connors was the great love of my young life and remains so for me still, as a person of warmth and sorrow, kindliness and fear, thoughtfulness and loneliness.

She is my Connacht lady, born where a violent queen cruised always in the back of the people's minds, for her maiden name was O'Malley and she was born within sight of Clare Island, and Grace O'Malley, pirate queen, her fortress, the still standing Granuaile's Clare Island fort. She grew up under the heavy presence of the Reek, the pyramid-shaped pilgrim mountain, Croagh Patrick, whose bruised sides rise steeply to the shrill demands of an old-fashioned western God. Boycott and Pearse she knew of, and De Valera hurt by stones on a lorry stage at Achill Sound, she knew those desperate World Wars to which she surrendered her sons a while, but those great storms of history ultimately passed on, leaving her with her faith, her love of family, her sorrows.

She sang to herself as she moved about the kitchen, I sitting in some corner, playing at something, but listening, absorbing who she was and what she was. I remember how, during those frequent nights of storm, she would cry for her son, Jim, who was out on those dreadful seas on his rickety ship, the winds coming screaming down our chimney as if to remind her of the dangers through which her beloved, errant son, was sailing. And I would suffer for her, too, when he returned, rarely enough, from some foreign port, for he returned in a slow skirl of alcohol, loving her, but unable to keep himself away from what he knew would inevitably hurt her deeply. She faced huge spaces in her prayers. And her other son, Jack, an alcoholic, too, a hero of the RAF during the Second World War, now living far from her in England. Times I could hear the sobbing from her room where I knew she would be kneeling by her bed, her prayers urgent for her boys, her heart shuddering now because her husband, Ted, Jack Connors, had died and left her alone to face such sorrows. Even as a young boy my heart hurt for her as she created her own histories, hearing the distant, cold silences of God. But she always stood strong and loving behind the black sky of an apron rich with tiny white stars, linen for the rubbing of her fingertips against the itch of grief.

Uncle Jim, ship's engineer. I stood with Nanna, both of us tensed and fidgeting, at Westport Station. The train came heavily round the long curve, and shuddered to a halt. I kept thinking it had come from terrible distances, Darwin, Cape Horn, the Ivory Coast. And there he was, stumbling on the platform, his eyes red, his breath foul. He came up to me, pretending not to notice his mother and whispered: 'Not a word to her, young sailor, not a word!' Nanna was already weeping, her fists pressed tightly against her head. She suffered, in silence, his fumbling, drunken kiss. And that night I heard her sobbing again in her room. I knew she would be twisting the beads between her fingers: 'and after this our exile, show unto us the blessed fruit of thy womb'.

She told me once, when Jim was young and innocent, that Ted in his carpentry shed had given him a coping-saw and glue, a breast-drill, plywood, plane, and he began at once to carve a Viking ship. He didn't make such a bad fist of it, she said, and then he floated it down the stream outside the gate. Jim sat and listened to the cries of gulls when they went to the beach, while others gathered stones for paperweights, those mantelpiece-perfect shells. When they watched the porpoises passing across the mouth of the bay, the ballet of their moving left him shaken. And then he, too, was at sea, moving through places like Rotterdam, Southampton, Brest; and to further places, Murmansk, Java, Singapore. She kept all the postcards he sent home, the stamps with angel butterflies, with native masks and birds of paradise. Once only he sent a photograph; he stands, blue-suited, groomed and moustached for his wedding; there is a bungalow on stilts behind him. And then the letter came, of his dying, his ship in flames while anchored in a distant harbour. His grave, they told her, is on high ground and bamboo canes shape a cross above him. Port Moresby, Papua New Guinea, her seafarer, her wanderer, home.

When Ted died, Nanna – whose days stretched back, as did his, to the nineteenth century – took charge of the mysteries, the joyful, the sorrowful, and the glorious. She had retired into blacks and greys, for out of darkness we come, she used to say, and into darkness we must go. Each night we knelt, the rules of recitation fixed. After the final 'glory' and 'amen', we settled into our own silences, our elbows hard against the hard seat of the wooden chair, our knees sore against the flagged floor, and we floated away into our privacies, into our prayers. I watched her face (as I yielded easily to any distractions), the old flesh, talced and spotted, her eyes closed and lifted, as if she could see beyond the darkness of our fall, to a bright redemptive country where those she had borne and loved would be walking again, unhurt, and Christ walking with them. I saw tears ease themselves onto her cheeks till her whispering prayers became for me the entire structure of the mysteries, the words and the Word, flesh distilled to grief and love, and all this gravity straining towards the invisible.

I missed a day or two at school; I had a sore throat, a genuine sore throat. Nanna fussed about me, the red light burning on the Pilot wireless, the world beyond, with its wars and winnowings, whistling to come in. I heard the monastery bell in the distance telling *angelus*; it was a special moment, never to be forgotten, something about harmony, about Nanna knocking her breast and announcing it aloud, *and the Word was made flesh*, and I, answering, heedlessly, *and dwelt amongst us*. And much later, this:

Dear Jackie:
I enclose a crisp new ten shilling note. Keep doing well at your studies. We have got the electric now and all the shadows have been vanishing from the house. I miss them. Bluebottles keep banging themselves off the hot bulbs in a misery of desire. The television set brings war and bad news in the door, and sometimes all you can see is something like snow, and all you can hear is a long, hissing sound. Then we turn the darn thing off. But once, on the radio long ago, I heard Count John McCormack singing at the Eucharistic Congress and then there was Canon Sidney MacEwan and he was singing 'Queen of the angels and Queen of the May' and we were even able to see him, and the bishops and priests and all, on the little screen. They are advertising everything imaginable that could be in the whole world and everyone is gone mad buying all sorts of things they never had need of before. I always pray,

Jackie, you will have a vocation. Turn your desires ever towards
God, all else leaves us in a stew. Pray for me.
Your own loving
Nanna

I can go back, quiet as a ghost, from where I am, back to where sweet
coals are whispering against the grate; I can go back, while hailstones
sputter against the panes outside – and see her standing in the doorway,
snow falling softly, an old woman's spotted apron holding her, and know
that she is watching too, ghosting inwards and going back, visiting her
losses, Ted, her sons, her daughter Patricia dead too young, much too
young, as if she could find a way to string all her life together, into a
sentence that might make some human sense, and I can sit remembering,
from where I am, and shaping in my memory that dusk her rosary burst
asunder and the beads went spilling skittering all-which-ways on the
stone-flagged floor of the kitchen as if her prayers and aspirations left
nothing in her shaking hands but a thread, bereft.

When she was through with them, the sheets
roistered on a sunbright day in off-the-Atlantic breezes;
Nanna washed them, there at the lake's edge, the water
a golden brown from the heather-hillside's leaching;
she trampled them in the sandy shallows, scrubbed
with a hard red soap and trampled them again;
sometimes she sang – holding long skirts up
in both hands – an air of maiden Ireland in her pains;
she stretched them out over a rock, or floated them
over the clover-speckled grass in an easing sun;
noon-time, on the high line, they were yawls,
spinnakers or topsails, sometimes clapping loud
at unexpected liberties. When I slept between them
they were elemental arms, holding me in her love.

She was woman, Nanna, grandmother, widow, carer. I loved her, and she
loved me with a pious and thoughtful loving. But she was tough, too; she
had to be, life having given her more than her share of pains and losses,

and a strong helping of God-fearing religious watchfulness. And yes, she knew all about death, and hens, and chickens; nor did she let pointless sentiment blind her to the needs of family and nourishment. I see her still; she carries a racketing old ash-bucket to the pit where she sieves out the dead day's waste and burning through the bucked riddle; I watch the sweet-silk ash-shuffle whispering where the grits and the blackened bones blow in last exposure to the winds; then, satisfied, she geeshes it all onto the heap. Nanna kept Rhode Island Red in a fenced-off patch of stones, with balded grass and scratchings; she threw in some food-refuse, parings, peels, carolling her chuck-chuck-chuck towards her care. I asked her if she had names for them, she seemed to like them so; and she only chuckled, No! *Give them names*, she said, *they will exhibit a personality of their own and then you might get to love them, and how on earth could you kill and eat them then?* I watched the hens, their mincing about, the auburn feathers gleaming gold sometimes, wet sometimes with the stain of emerald. At times, then, she would grab one in her left hand, hold it sphincter-over-head by the yellow-leather wrinkled boniness of the claws, and lay its neck across a wooden block. I saw the fluttering of wings, the raisin-eye wide open, till she brought the hatchet down with a rude thud. The body flapped in her hand, then slackened, and fell still, a tiny rain of blood spattering on her kitchen apron. After days the claws were all that would be left to the riddle, gold-gleams in there among the ashes.

She was always old, grandmother, Nanna; sea-sorrow had made her so. Arms across her breasts, she was leaning back against the sun-warmed rocks, at Bunafahy, Dooega, Achill Island. She was tired in black, as the rocks are, with their ancient lichens swathing them. Easy waves came reaching onto the strand while children's calls were lost amidst the cries of gulls. A patch of the high field across the road was glistening under sun, as the world offers, sometimes, small glistenings of joy though there are shelves of tritest stuff no tide will cover. In the water there were pulsings of unwarranted jellyfish, as if the ocean itself were pulsing. Sister death – idling and almost visible in the rougher waves offshore – was always close to her as her two lost sons, her fingertips bruised from too much telling of the beads, it being sure that Jesus-Prospero had told no end to sorrow in this life. Now, as I was watching her, she was watching the white ocean-fingers writing words onto the sand. And much later, this:

Dear Jackie:

Thanks for your always welcome letter. It's as ever good to hear from you, I know you can write only once a month. I take up my pen now to tell you all is well and quiet here, DG. Father Tiernan has complained off the altar about the dance hall back the road. The monastery in Bunnacurry is being closed. Doesn't that say something about the times that are in it? The foxes have been in the chicken-run again. The travellers are back and are camping just outside the old quarry. I am lonesome, between times. I have not been feeling all that well, pains in my chest, tiredness. Pray for me …

Dearest Nanna

You'd laugh to see me, sometimes, ring the seminary bell to announce angel-time, or festival High Mass. I have to swing my weight on the long rope, three draws without a muttering from the bell, building-up, like preparation for prayer, and then a surge and I'm hoisted high, the bell calling, I in flight, like Icarus, three times three and nine, a music ever-so-slightly off its key, but it brings me back to Bunnacurry grove when I'd climb, grandchild among the pine-trees towards the windy top and sit, part of it, and then the chapel bell would ring the Angelus and three or four minutes later the bell from the monastery would call and I'd see you, there in the yard, praying, you'd strike your breast and the Word was made flesh and you'd genuflect and hold yourself, head bowed, a long time in reflection. I think of those times a great deal. Sometimes the memories make me sad, but mostly I am very happy here, and pray for you every day. Pray for me …

She spent her last few weeks in the hospice, not far from the seminary, and I called in whenever I could get permission. She didn't seem to be in pain, but she was very confused. At times she did not know who I was and other times she simply called me 'Father': I was wearing my black suit, clerical collar, and black hat when I arrived. The room was filled with sunlight. A great bowl of flowers stood just inside the window. There was a pleasing silence and I felt she was at peace. But once, while I was sitting quietly at her bedside, she sat up suddenly, gazed to the foot of the bed, started to speak, though the words, slurred and hurried, made

no sense to me. She was somewhat animated, she looked pleased. I was
not frightened; with Nanna, there was never any other sense than one of
love and kindliness and peace.

> She died;
> I stood over her plot
> in stole and surplice
> sprinkling water,
> holding myself detached
> in sacred ceremony, as if love
> could not have scope
> and human tears were failure;
> Nanna, treasure in heaven;
> childhood over
> and the dim ages, my eyes
> opening.

*Achill, the Island*

Where bogland hillocks hid a lake
we placed a tom-cat on a raft; our guns
clawed pellets in his flesh until, his back
arched, the pink tongue bitten through, he drowned.
We fished for gulls with hooks we'd hide
in bread and when they swallowed whole we'd pull;
screaming they sheared like kites above a wild
sea; twine broke and we forgot. Until
that day we swam where a great shark
glided past, dark and silent power
half-hidden through swollen water; stunned
we didn't shy one stone. Where seas lie calm
dive deep below the surface; silence there
pounds like panic and moist fingers touch.

In my early years on Achill Island, the basking shark swimming right into Keem Bay was a fairly regular sight. Over the years it was netted and slaughtered for its oils and its blubber. The golden eagle has long been absent from the slopes of the mountain, Slievemore. Now only the wheatears can be heard, scolding from the edges of rocks high above. Sometimes, too, the hooded crow will let out a deep-throated craaawrk, or a rare chough will pitch its high scream across the air. By another low cliff there is a patch of turf sunk between field and cove, where neglected, rough slabs are uninscribed, marking where the unbaptised were locked away in unblessed cells, hustled lives whom neither God nor devil coveted. They were buried here by night, in secret, in unbearable sorrow, telling of harsh times and a Deity of whom the word 'love' could never have been used. 'Killeen'; 'cillín', little church, little burial place: where familiar and unknown worlds touch in the clay beneath; children, lifted out from blood-confusion, put aside where sea-smoothed stones lie over them; our sad fathers, our sad fathers. Some distance away from this field of grief there is a high rampart of rounded stones that separates a salt marshland from the salt Atlantic; to go clambering up that rampart was to take five steps forward and four steps back. But at last you stood where the Atlantic wind snatched away your breathing, breakers coming in *crescendo* into *rallentando*, and you could stand for hours, taken and mesmerised by the majesty of it, the wonder, the everlasting movement of the ocean, and grow aware of your own small living, the tininess of human being, the unwarranted surging of human pride.

Love, I believed, was like starting on a pilgrimage, stepping blithely out over the gunwale, hoping to waltz on water; there would be hands working inside one another's lives, grasping the heart for hold. Then there was mother, father, there was the island, the island edges, the storms, the seas, the summer days along the strand. I heard their voices through the wall, at night, just like summer murmuring. At times, he brought her honeycombs in wooden frames soft as the host, and a small, hard ball of wax lingered in the mouth after the sweetness. Now in the photograph they are still striding out together along the beach, smiling, confident, striding into the confusion of their final months, their love a bonding, though dulled later on and unspoken; they will disappear, exemplary, together, as if the sea had swallowed them, but they will leave echoes of a low, ongoing music.

Perhaps God is not the shore on which, like grounded boats, we end our pilgrimage; perhaps God is the ocean we step out on through death into our origins.

Spring-tide has left our foreshore littered
with topknot, turbot, dogfish, squid,
with goby, scorpion, sand-eel, plaice,
barnacle, bristle-tail, beetle, brill,
paddock, oyster, periwinkle, trough,
hermit, sea hare, sea slug, star,
the man-o'-war, by-the-wind-sailor,
dead men's fingers, chinaman's hat,
potato, cucumber, lumpsucker, squirt;
sea-words floundering between the teeth,
mouthful, salt on the tongue, and spume.


I crept up to the resinous loft, at times, in the chapel, Bunnacurry, where Mother reigned; the schoolgirls gathered by her, their hair, their scent, and oh how they huddled together, watching me, derisively. The priest, on the altar, took his cue from her, and from that breathless harmonium, the diapason, the celeste. I remember – there by the pamphlet rack, by the window ledge – the unclaimed glove, the beads, the sacred medal, such things lying with a few dead and dying flies, and how that darkwood staircase to the loft came to be a heaviness in my blood, a dare to my spirit. And the Protestants, oh how strange their names, like Sidebotham, like all those colours, Mrs Black, Violet Gray, Mrs White. How strange, too, that they lived in a colony, apart; their minister wore grey pullovers and had a wife!

I watched, once, as Miss Constance Brown called; she made flowers out of pipe-cleaners and coloured crepe; black lace gloves reached above her elbows. Mother bought a few flowers from her for, she said, the Protestants are down on their luck. I remember one black rose that she bought and hid it away behind the picture of Our Lady; then, when the house was sold, there was a pale rectangle left on the wall and one small, mourning, petal. But our place was an island, and our lives were island lives; God was another, distant island and bore no real or meaningful relationship to anything we did on our place. We had few pleasure-boats back then, because life was not for pleasure but for hardship; our fishing crafts were heavy and efficient, the priest blessed them, they were given names like prayers. Maris Stella. Ave Maria. I remember how I learned to play long lines out over the gunwales in a carnival of feathers; mackerel shoals were driving past beneath us, hunting sprat; a furious hunger theirs, and ours, not to be satiated.

Winters were true winters on my island. When the lake froze over we were Breughel's villagers, rag-tag and bulky, skating across a little, temporary Eden. Even Father seemed to regain a childhood innocence, the ends of a scarf lifting behind him like wings. I skimmed stones across the surface of the lake and heard them sing out of their dullness, it was like listening to strings being plucked on an untuned fiddle. As we tried to skate, our breathing hovered on the air about us like guardian, seraph angels. All year round, down certain roads, dogs hurled themselves against the wheels of cars. Along the shore curraghs lay, over winter, face down under ropes and stones in the way the gossamer soul is baulked by bone. Late spring, we whittled turves into shapes of house or woman or animal, then set them up along the turf banks to dry, but the sun shrivelled them and they were sods of turf again, ready for the burning.

In Purteen harbour they were gutting fish; the men stood, blood-spattered yellow waders reaching to the waist, their red hands swollen from the killing. Entrails, fish-heads, floated on the tide and only the summer ray, lifted for a while from their element into ours and flung back, useless, to sink, stunned and airlocked, to the harbour floor, seemed to come alive again, back from the dead; I watched them rise slowly, out of death-trance and move, softly as dreams, back towards the ravenous sea.

It was late afternoon. I was supposed to be sitting over my books at the kitchen table, catechism lesson, a few sums ... But I was idling at the window and I remember being puzzled over a crucifix that was hanging to the side of the mantelpiece, the figure on the Cross unnaturally thrusting to one side, as if in a vast and awful spasm of pain. I had little sense, then, of how much the human being suffers, of how much the human being, he or she, is capable of suffering. And I was bemused, too, how the wood of the crucifix, that looked to me like a contorted small branch of a hawthorn bush, appeared to be twisted alongside its burden. Just then a man I knew from down the village came cycling past our house, coming from the direction of Cashel, and turned down the road towards his home. The afternoon was grey; there had been rain, there would be more. I saw how the handlebars of the bike suddenly twisted to one side and bike and man fell over onto the loose-stone side of the road. I was startled, a little frightened, for the man, for his fall. But he gathered himself up rather quickly, and gathered up the bike, too, though he almost fell over on top of it before he got it upright. I could see him hesitate, then decide he would push the bike up the slight incline and not attempt to ride it. I could see his hair blowing like straw-wisps in the breeze; I saw his hand on the chrome bar of the bike, big and knuckled and fierce. He staggered as he began to walk, holding the bike out from him lest it buck like a wild ass, and kick him. He was drunk! I knew it at once, for it was not the first time I had seen this man fall about the place, even in the middle of the afternoon.

He moved cautiously now, though he could not hold a straight line along the road. At last I saw him stop again, having reached the top of the incline. He mounted, warily, like a cowboy in our old films who would try to tame an unbroken stallion. He got himself on the saddle and the bicycle moved, shakily, forward, veering eerily from side to side, the man's long brown coat flapping against the cross-bar, striking against the spokes of the back wheel, his route now the longest distance between points. I held my breath as the bike gathered speed and suddenly he was heading for the left-hand side of the road; he cycled straight off and down into the drain, falling, bike and all, tumbling backside over bars into what was a deep and wet drain down below Lineen's stores. In the long interval before his resurrection onto the road – before he abandoned the bike and headed off, still staggering, relying on the safer use of his own limbs – I remember turning to that twisted figure on the crucifix and knowing that my heart and soul uttered a prayer that was probably one of the truest prayers I have said in my life. Many, many years later I remembered that man as I stood before a painting in the church in Orvieto, Italy, Signorelli's masterful 'Resurrection of the Flesh', where naked humans are climbing stiffly out of the soil, some of them still reduced to their twisted skeletons, answering the calling trumpets of the angels.

Ours was the house at the crossroads. Early every morning, about 7 o'clock, the bus from Dooagh at the end of the island, passed our crossroads on its way to Westport and the trains. Once I woke to a disturbed dimness; I could sense the simperings of drifting rain outside, the early-morning breezes in the pines. Before I had fallen asleep the night before, I had heard the sounds of a cart coming towards our gate, the gate being opened, then the murmurings of voices and I knew that a trunk, or suitcases, had been left for safe-keeping and in readiness, inside our gate. By the time I awoke the next morning, it had already begun, the creaking of a cart, the slow-rhythm, dull, steady hoof-beats of a horse, coming from the village to intercept the bus outside our gate. Then I could hear them, those urgent, hushed voices, those nervous shiftings against the darkness.

A woman's voice lifted high in a wail of distress, like a small furred animal transfixed. Then I was wide awake to the sound of the approaching bus, its labouring through the gears towards a stop. I heard the sorry ticking sound it made while it paused on its journey. I could imagine the trunk, bulked and new, tied round perhaps with fishing-rope, how it would be hoisted up onto the roof of the bus and covered over with tarpaulin. Then I heard those awkward voices, I imagined the gestures of held-back sorrow, of loss and of despair, I sensed the embarrassed kisses and hugs, the knobbled words like sand ramparts against a surging tide, I knew how the hurt would be pushed back, the way one holds one's hands to one's side to contain the suffering. And then the bus moved, loudly, labouring on the road, diminishing at last into silence. Silence. Then the creaking of a cart, the same, slow rhythmic plod of the hoof-beats of a horse.

We reach our hands upwards in supplication; ours is the posture of ignorant attending, the forked tree, the fists flung out in surrender.

> He breaks the host, I hear the breast-bone
> of a small bird snapping; he hoists the sweet-
> blood chalice, I hear cries of distress
> from a famished people. When we enter
>
> it is the stone terminus of an underground
> and we wait, in ranks, sway, sigh and leave
> as if we had reached a destination. He
> was broken, taken down, buried, and grew
>
> whole again and won authority over this
> flawed creation. Give us this day our daily
> incentives; fill us with goals though there is
> no goal; give us this day our energy.
>
> O broken God be with us always
> now, and to the end of time.

*Miscellany: The Rhododendron Wood*

Those early days of childhood and childishness had something to do with trees, not the great individual trees: oak, sycamore, or elm for these are serious trees, serious about the business of growing high and powerful, like human beings intent on growing into the bullying and intense living of adulthood, but I am thinking of the bushes that grew closer to the level of a child's shoulder and to the magic of his hiding-places, small groves of rhododendron, fuchsia, thorn. It is greatly important to a child that he or she find places in which to lurk, to be free of adult supervision and adult rules, and to soar in imagination through territories of complete freedom and wonder. And the low shrubbery that can yet conceal a small body is ideal for such imaginings. Such shrubs and bushes offer hidden spaces with clay floors beaten hard and smooth where you can draw the leaf and blossom about you like walls; they offer hidden pathways around formal fields and meadows where you can crawl, unseen, and watch and mock the adult ordinances; and they present the possibilities of a kind of prayer, a communion with creation herself on a word-less level, in an intimate relationship unspoiled by the heavier thoughts of adulthood survival.

On Achill Island I found many such places, glorious dens far from the madding crowd, in which I could skulk, and live, and become whatever I wanted to be. In the wilder places, on the low hills, there were clumps of thorn bushes, places of spine and blossom and of contorted limb; the wonder was of that gold-bloom, the bird-feathers caught on the furze, the blood-flakes and sun-stain on the blossom. Here you could hide, listening to the sky filling up with the music of the morning lark. Here you could skulk and imagine all sorts of wonderful revenge, against the big-fisted bullies whom you could, in dreams, punish seriously while you hid, in here on the earth hardened over roots, in a den fragrant and cool, among thorns, where the foolish adults would least expect to find you. And there is, in the Bible, the great story of the prophet Elijah who, finding himself weary with his long journeys and his exhortations, found himself a furze bush, stretched out his body in its embrace and wished that his life were dust.

Achill Island is rich in the profusion of its fuchsia bushes, with those wondrous blood-red flowers we called the Tears of God. I cycled down a lane between such bushes, I fell off my bike and cut my knee, all pride washing out of me in tears and the 'tut-tut-tut' of the nurse. When I left the doctor's house I stood abashed amongst the fuchsia, a new white bandage on my knee, a scrape along my palm which I could later display proudly to my class. But I found comfort in climbing into the row of fuchsia bushes, in staying quite hidden there while squeezing onto my wrist the tiny drops of nectar that the blossoms offered. As if nature herself, in her bounty, could wipe away all tears and offer in their place the generous opulence of honey.

And then there was the rhododendron wood that ran through an old estate on Achill, a place apart, a mystery where a retired Major lived, a presence of mythology and lore, an exotic and a danger amongst our lowland places. Taking, as I thought, my life in my hands, I left the bike in a ditch and climbed a fence into his wood. At once, as it was evening, the treetops lifted in a racketing of starlings and I knew a surge of guilt, its shivering excitement. I crept along the rhododendron hedgerows, across the ancient littering of its leaves and blossoms, and it brought me right to the edge of the outhouses. I came out from the bushes and at once big cattle came, lurching towards me like an audience, quizzical and eager to be pleased. I peered through a high window of the big house, into other worlds, there was a salon with great mirrors, there were antlers hung on the wall alongside plaques of old gallantry and privilege. I felt islanded beyond my own island, outside, alien and alone. Skulking as I was, close to the gentry of old Ireland, when the Irishry were oppressed and their children hungry. And when a door opened suddenly nearby, the fear I knew made me shiver through my body and speed back, fast as a lizard, into the safe arms of the rhododendrons.

These gifts of nature, these arthritic twigs, this spittle of sap-flow and rising, all the leaves and blossoms and the untamed green of the sheltering places, are rich in the sensuous movements of the winds, rich in memory and imagination as if they were places where you could find the perfect cell, the desert solitary places. These were my days and I accepted them, times when the days hung heavy and time appeared irrelevant, and all of it the closeness in the blood of the most beautiful aspects of a beautiful nature. As the poet Gerard Manley Hopkins wrote: Long live the weeds and the wilderness yet.

*That Man*

Long summer evenings, after the dust and dullness of his work, Father would set out from Purteen harbour and stride on over rock and cliff-edge towards the far headland where he loved to fish. There was exhilaration in the lark's song high above the fields, in the seagulls' cries from out over the waves. The mossy ground was soft, the turfy slopes, the hillocks; fishing-rod in his hand, a song in his soul. Slugs spread themselves out before his feet, but he avoided them, passing by the cove where things were festering down in the cold dark. From the furthest point of rock he would fish. Pollock, heavy as stone, flabby as seaweed, he landed unwillingly; he put his fingers into the gills and snapped the back; he would slap the body from his man's height down onto the rocks. When the mackerel shoaled, coming in around the headland in a fountain of silvery spray and the sprat tried to fly out of the boiling water to escape them, then his heart exulted, and his body trembled with excitement.

'This is the way towards kindness'
he said, 'believe me', and I did;
I saw the small brown flecks of wisdom
like rust-drops on his hands;
six blind, sleek, mewling kittens

birth-wet and innocent of claw,
he gathered into a hessian bag
with stones for travelling companions
and swung and swung it through the blue air
and out into the water of the lake.

Sometimes still I see them scrabbling,
their snout-heads raised, their bodies
nude and shivering in an alien element,
sometimes – when I see the children,
their big, wide-open eyes unseeing,

skin stretched dry and crinkling
like leather and above them the blue sky,

that enviable sun shining – again I hear
'this is the way towards kindness,
believe me' and I do, I do, I do.

I stood, reaching my hand up to grasp his hand; over the island the night sky was vast, star after star drawing my face upwards, the depths, and silence, his silence answering. He hoisted me onto a plinth of bog earth where I was lost suddenly, and afraid, watching the star sheen on his face. And once I was with him, walking the silken zig-zag trace of the waves where spume from the sea was blowing in on us like snow; he was big, then, bigger than weather, and everlasting. Later, much later, I watched black clouds gathering against the broad shoulder of Cruaghan; he was old now, but he was out in the waves off Keem Bay, swimming; I saw him stumble, and fall and I reached to help, to hoist his body upright. The sea had water-coloured his flesh blue and scarlet and indigo; there were few words left between us, there at the sea's edge, to loose the knotted thing that had grown within me, for I had not learned to name it, 'love', nor to display it, 'care'; slight, shivering father, star-particle, pelt.

You came into the game from a starting-point near rocks and ran, trying to reach the stone placed at the centre, the den, the safehouse, home. And there I go – a child still in the game – screaming round the outermost circle, father pounding after, a switch of sea-wrack in his hand. Eternity, he told me, is like the letter O, it has no beginning and no end, or like the naught, perhaps, and you could slither down and down through its black centre. With a silver pin he drew the periwinkles from their shells, soft flesh uncoiling from the whorl; he scooped out gravelly meat from the barnacle, swallowed its roundness whole, with the black mucous-like blob at its centre. And there I go, half-nauseated, still following; the way you become your father, that same diffidence and turning inwards, that same curving of the spine, the way the left shoulder lifts in emphasis; and here I am, pounding round the outermost circle, a switch of sea-wrack in my hand.

A small row-boat on Keel Lake,
the water sluppering gently as he rowed,
the easy sh-sh-sshhhh of the reeds

as we drifted in, and all about us
tufts of bog-cotton like white moths,
the breathing heathers, that green-easy lift

into the slopes of Slievemore. All else
the silence of islands, and the awe
of small things wonderful: son,

father, on the one keel, the ripples
lazy and the surfaces of things unbroken.
Then the prideful swish of his line

fly-fishing, the curved rod graceful,
till suddenly mayfly were everywhere,
small water-coloured shapes like tissue,

sweet as the host to trout and – by Jove!
he whispered, old man astounded again
at the frenzy that is in all living.

He taught me God, without insisting, and God became all gentleness, a
life. We dug for worms in the vegetable field; he stooped over the spade
in concentration, they uncoiled coiled about each other in his tin tobacco
box. Then we sat together on the riverbank, patient and watching, close
to the pulsing by of the world. To be pierced like that and hung
midstream, out of the natural element! so that now my mind revolts at it,
revolts too at the face that peers absorbed over its purposes – his gentle
hands drawing the fleshly shape over the hook like a glove, we two
hunched in voluntary cruelty – and I saw God too lean leering out over
the rim of the world, absorbed. Later still I watched him, stooped at last
over himself, sitting in the ward, alone, and absent; he was labouring to
admit God's hands drawing his flesh onto pain like a glove, suspended
in the gullet between life and death; I could not intrude, I prayed him
grace and he came back wearied from his far country; it was the dying of
the old man, the ego hung midstream, out of the natural element. We are,
as if we are forever; our passage will be difficult; when it comes at last
that we are other, dumb and senseless, presiding out of photographs or
from a book, the terrible angel at the gate will ask of us what we have
done for the gratification of the world. Can you accept death in advance

of death? Can you accept that the Christ, though he is dead, may walk our streets, disheartened, jostled, or out along the marsh road, calling and ignored?

Evening rain came in gusts off the Atlantic. Father locked the office door behind him: cabbage green paint like scabs on sunburnt skin; locking himself away a while from tedium. Tang of sea-rot on the air; it would be easy, self-pitying, to lift the mind towards God. The Morris Minor waited, glum and heavy; he choked it, rain all day persisting. He gripped the driving wheel, moved, cautiously, across the yard and out towards the road. Sluggish, this afternoon, self and car. Don. Donal. Daniel Patrick Deane. Turn right for Alice's Harbour Bar. Left, for home. He knows the sickening frisson of excitement: to be caulked in companionable darkness, drink comforting, the world shaping itself to manageable forms.

We, at home, waiting. The gut tightening. Long past time. Clock on the mantel ticking a little more loudly. Sensing how it rounds again, like the tide. [Nights, he drew the curtains, sealing us in a yellow light; Bela, he told us, means beautiful, and she – So our matt-painted walls became the steppes, the black impossible eyes of a woman flared at us, we saw the flanks of horses gleaming in the moonlight. Broad is the river Dnieper, he told us, the proud wild goose glides swiftly over. Sometimes we shivered as Mephistopheles approached, or when we heard Carmen's lovely laughter: *la fleur que tu m'avais jetée dans ma prison* ... How could we know, as we nestled down to sleep, the nightmare of the tedium of his days?]

The window of Alice's Harbour Bar watches out over the sound, the glass grimed with the spittle of wind and sea. In the gloom the man's big fist gripped the pint of stout, his feet found purchase on the sawdust floor. We are dust, he'd say, we're built of dust and will collapse back into dust. Alice has laughed her gruff, considerate laugh; has seen it all before, and heard, the thirst, the colander emptiness being filled, and she has held them, their strong hands trembling, their minds grown friable as dried-out clay, their drowning cries audible to everyone but themselves.

> There! amongst lean-to grasses and trailing vetch
> catch her? – vagrant, free-range and alert;
>
> I saw the eager watch-tower of the ears, I knew
> the power of legs that would fling her into flight;

concentrate, he said, and focus: you must love
the soft-flesh shoulder-muscles where the bullet bites,

caress – and do not jerk – the trigger: be all-embracing, be
delicate. I had no difficulty with the saucepan lid

down at the end of the meadow, lifted, for practice,
against the rhododendron hedge, I could sight

its smug self-satisfaction and shoot a hole
pea-perfect and clean through. Attention to the hare

left me perplexed for I, too, relish the vision
I imaged in its round dark eye, of a green world

easy under sunlight, of sweet sorrel and sacred herbs –
and I turned away, embarrassed, and absolved.

Northwards the rain was brushing grey over the world; westwards there was distance, black impasto clouds. In the blunt Ford Prefect smelling of oil, tobacco, I held the big, moulded driving wheel; around us the obstacles were sheep, and hare-track culverts; my future was there, beyond the dashboard, out over the bonnet, a huge and virgin canvas. Father, straight-backed, tender and patient, held my fingers on the wheel; it was noon, there was stillness, it was the first day of the world.

Now he is still gazing out the rear window, over sand-dunes, strand and waves, the skin of his face finger-applied out of limed clay; God's image, in waistcoat and shirt, the small stud dangling. Still life. While far away, in the background, a milk-white gannet is diving into the sea. And then I see him: he has been moving on the widening circumference of a circle of his own making; eye bright, back straight, and head erect; his shirt-sleeves folded well above the elbow, sweat on his flesh, intoxicating clover-pollen rising to him and the high grass – in breathless ballet – falling at his feet. He has achieved a rhythm that takes him from us for a while, his soul a hub of quietness, his body melting into the almost perfect elliptical orbiting of the world, the scythe sharp as razors, his swinging of it a music in itself. Soon he will flop down tiredly amongst us, his thoughts turning on the heroes of myth and literature while the grass at the centre of his circle has begun, imperceptibly, to green.

I watched him, hooked over the kitchen table,
the instruments of his heart's desire
ranged before him: tweezers, dubbin, vise;
materials – feathers, threads, fluffs and beads;
such colours, amaranth, carnelian, saffron, taupe;
the delicacy, like down of thistle, like catkin-milt;
and the hidden hooks, to dazzle a watery eye, and all
worked between thick and nicotine-stained fingers.
He opened out his folding wallet, his treasury of flies,
richness beyond delight, all beautiful and murderous.
Outside, a shower of rain was darkening the day
though a feeble sun already groped through clouds.
I, too, inveigled, though on a lesser scale, in my way
searching the world's presence for its pulse and throb;
the vegetable garden, after rain, yielded its lush
pink-red worms I gathered in to his old tobacco tin.
Dusk, and he was wading into the lake, the fishing-rod
long and whip-lean, and he would swish and curl
the fleshly-coloured line onto the water, the chosen flies
vivid as if they lived; I, with stump-rod, twine and worm
sat by the river pool, watched the cork, dreamed
and – impatient at his patience – slapped at midges.
Who has long gone into the anima mundi, rest
I hope, for the soul, spent from recurring storms,
the spirit-wallet filled with all good things, peace
for the flesh from the flesh's urge, to be and to be
more than it may be here: clay, and thread, bright
gaud and hook, and inevitable disappointment.

Darkness. Wind about the house brushing against our walls. I could sense, through shut eyelids, the lighter shade of curtains between the blacknesses within and those without.

In the new suburbs there are no trees to soften the winds and to give them names. We huddle among painted bricks and rafters, alarms primed to scream, hoping the foliage will grow, quickly, round us.

I folded my body up under the electric blanket. The wind, not animal, tore clematis from the garden walls, knocked down the sweet, red-painted, bird-tables. After a time I slept.

Old man naked. Laid on a farmhouse kitchen table, on thick, scrubbed timbers. His long body the colour of sour cream. His hands along the timbers, raw, at his sides. The chest-hair thick, grey-white. The face, inscrutable, as always. Vague figures shifting round him, presences, unnamed. I see the wild and wintering grey-lag, shot.

Again. I stand above. Down below, a patch of earth. Black clay. Cleared ground. Huddled at a distance, in heavy coats, halt, people. Indistinct, but shocked. Old man naked. The body whiter than known white. Lying at the edge of the earth, at an angle. Knees drawn up, birthing, hands raised above the head, pleading innocence. I see the wild and wintering grey-lag, shot. Soon, I wake.

He was sitting at the foot of a bed, on a high, hospital chair. I noticed the steel end of the bed, the steel handle, like the cranking-handle of an old Ford Prefect. The sheets rigid with white, the counterpane, light-blue, smoothed out. He was sitting perfectly still, hands on his lap, head lowered. The pink, bare skull, the few white hairs on the nape of the neck. The collar of his dressing-gown had one side folded in on itself. Small tufts of hair in his ear.

Old man. Exposed to the wildering rush of the current.

He was turned at an angle from me, motionless. And knowing. He had taken himself already a great distance from the ward. I was reluctant to bring him back. Through the wide, hospital window, the rough seashore of rooftops. I touched him on the shoulder. He turned his face towards me, gathering himself back out of his preparations. And looked. My own, tense face, staring, unseeing, up at me. Frightened. Tear-full. The hands, reaching upwards, for hold.

*On Another Shore*

the worn-out Otherthing
rigid on its slab, the fluids
stagnant;
dressed-up and parcelled – the Offence;

someone had set a plastic rose
upon the chest,
and we, attendants,
faces unmasked by grief

murmured our studied words:
he is not dead, but sleeping,
he is not here,
he has stepped out on another shore

beautiful beyond belief;
and we have crept back out
into weakened sunshine,
knowing our possibilities

diminished.


*On This Shore*

they laid him on his back
in the flat-bottomed
ramshackle boat that the dead use
and carried him down to the shore;

quickly he sank
into the current's hold
and did not come up again for air;
when I had kissed his forehead

he was already cold
and had begun to sweat;
soon he will have shed all baggage,
the great gannet of life

will be gliding over him like a dream;
he has cast off at last

from the high white cross
to which he was anchored

and I have turned back,
carrying his burden,
leaving a deeper set of footprints
across the sand.


*Riverdown*

It begins somewhere high in the hills, somewhere impossible to pinpoint with complete accuracy, the way the soul begins, perhaps, the way hope might begin, or faith. There must be a source, a wellspring, fed with the many rains that come in off the Atlantic and cross the island like spirits on some great migration. It begins as little more than a dribble out of peatlands, out of innocent places, marshy hollows, from under the high mist-clouds that take over these heather uplands where sheep shrug out shelters for themselves against bogbanks and cower low from the winds that pass through all the way from the frozen wastes thousands of miles away. The water comes to trickle out of mossy places, under the secret tracks of foxes and the rending-places of the hooded crow. Slowly it gathers, forging its tiny gorge, invisible at first, then gurgling so that you can hear it, like a presence somewhere in the darkness of night, and then it is found making its way down towards the white-washed gable-ends of outhouses.

It becomes a stream, almost before you are aware of it, where wheatears thrive along its margins and little golden eels find their living in it, hiding under half-buried stones and in under the dripping banks. It swells, the way a young life swells, garnering strength and a little pride in itself. Until it touches one of the old roads, manmade and inhibiting, where a bridge is built, where a child can crouch and hide, touch the flaking masonry of the underarch, be lonely and at peace, listening to the occasional car passing over. It is a place to listen to the small murmurings of the stream, to the jittering calls of the wren; it is a place, solitary there under the bridge, to stay forever, perfect, useless, desire stilled. A place, too, where a child can drop a tiny stick on one side of the bridge and run to watch it emerge on the other side, can know a small triumph, the learning of the forces that make this earth of ours continue on its way, a triumph as if a victory has been won, as if a three-masted schooner has been launched, successfully, into the flow.

But the stream moves on, without waiting; it moves through more human sounds, by the edges of a village, through cultivated fields, deepening all the time, the landscape flattening out and becoming dull, the river, for now it is a river, deepening betimes to a pool where small brown trout hold their bodies against the flow. Now it is time for the wandering child, absent from the flurries of what too many people call the real world, to stop and hear the distant bell from the monastery call out Angelus, announce noon, the turning point, the angel-mystery where, in the time of man's believing, a small genuflection would be made and people would touch their knee, humbly, to the sustaining earth.

Too soon the afternoon takes on its own breadth and greyness; all the rivers of the world flow down into the sea and yet the sea will not overflow. Admire, here, by the river that works to be called majestic, the beautiful bog-iris, the furze-bush blossomings, the rushes thriving in the marsh acres; now and then a donkey brays, or cows plash into muddying water. Nearer the sea there are houses, some old and rickety in the winds, some squat and new and scarcely lived in; dogs bark, and you are forced to climb out of the river's way into someone's meadow. Your pilgrimage down from high places has begun to weary you, because the pleasure has been in the travelling and now the tide has reached upriver, turning the world to slobland with its stench of decay, its mud-bubbles, mullet sluppering in the shallows and your spring has vanished into sea-rot. Still, you have grown knowledgeable, something has been achieved, you gather yourself still for the ongoing endeavour, you hold onto your longing that you will yet find the centre and source, the life-force, the mystery, home.

## *That Woman*

I was born within sight of Croagh Patrick, our pilgrim mountain, pyramid-shaped, with that little bump on the top that is a church, visible on clear days, away in a cobalt-blue haze against the brightness of the sky. I often saw the men and women leave our island, cycling, or on the morning bus, heading – some thirty-five miles – for Westport and on out the several more miles to the base of the mountain. They would climb, a difficult and sometimes dangerous climb, to the summit, many of them making the ordeal tougher by going up in their bare feet; up above, they would pray, then make the difficult descent, take their bikes, or the bus, and head for home. Some two and a half hours up, some two and a half hours down.

### *Penance*

They leave their shoes, like signatures, below;
above, their God is waiting. Slowly they rise
along the mountainside where rains and winds go
hissing, slithering across. They are hauling up

the bits and pieces of their lives, infractions
of the petty laws, the little trespasses and
sad transgressions. But this bulked mountain
is not disturbed by their passing, by this mere

trafficking of shale, shifting of its smaller stones.
When they come down, feet blistered and sins
fretted away, their guilt remains and that black
mountain stands against darkness above them.

Mother was pious, grandmother Nanna even more so. Father, too, in his way. But we were never taken to do that climb, and often I wonder why. We said the rosary every night; we went to all the sacraments, regularly, following the seasons of the Church. But we never took on the penance of Croagh Patrick. Perhaps there remained, somewhere deep down in their souls, a certain realism, or perhaps it was a fear that we children might not be able for it. But some hour and a half away from us, by car, there was Knock and in that little village, it was told, on the evening of 21 August 1879, Mary the Virgin, with St Joseph and St John the Evangelist appeared at the rough gable of the little church, there, in that village. There appeared, alongside them, an altar with a cross and the figure of a lamb, with angels hovering about them. Some fifteen witnesses, young and old, came forward to give testimony, and they watched there, and prayed for a long time. There were 'commissions of enquiry' set up, in 1879 and again in 1936, and the testimony of these witnesses was taken as trustworthy. Knock became one of the world's major Marian shrines. And it was here we went, several times, driving there by car, often when there was an official 'pilgrimage' announced. I always found it difficult. It seemed to rain every time. We walked round and round the church, reciting rosaries. I was young; I was bored. But I behaved, Mother insisting. Afterwards there was Mass in the little church, with sermon, singing, and Benediction. I did not like it. Not at all.

> We trudged round and round the old building
> as if we were getting somewhere, our fingers
> rambling round the beads, our heads
> bowed against the petulant winds and rains.
>
> We were an ancient people, our hearts
> full of ancient gentility, unlovely
> butterflies seeking a flame to burn against.
> The end wall of the church, we were told,
>
> and the inhospitable landscapes of the west
> had flared with a heavenly light. We have since
> learned to scoff at all such drollery, at the stalls
> rife with the junk of old piosity. Today
>
> ours is a swift, a rectilinear glide,
> to wealth, wellbeing and ultimate contentment.
> Sometimes I wonder, when that old, dim message
> of peace and love and prayer and charity

fades under the groans of stalled traffic, if perhaps
the perfect pilgrimage is a circling,
or better yet a wilful stomping in place,
or best of all, eyes closed, attending, and standing still.

Mary Josephine Deane, née Connors, Jo-Jo, strict Roman Catholic, with whom I fought, whom I loved deeply in my own way. I was young enough, I remember, to be allowed rummage in the big room, where the window looked out over the world towards the languid sea at Bunnacurry Pier. I could stand in the window recess those days, draw the curtains and be invisible. I touched the unguents and oils on the dressing table, the combs and brushes, the talc, mysteries to me, all of them. Sometimes I saw her face like a ghost's face smeared with cream. Later I came to know she must have sat, often, before the big, hinged mirror, watching through that window towards another life where she waltzed at the sea's edge, where the moon was an orange over palm trees. I could fancy her turning back, then, towards the mirror and wiping the moisture from about her eyes.

For her life could not have been easy; her father, Ted, strict and bullying; both of her brothers alcoholics, and then, later on, an alcoholic husband. Her sister, Patricia, whom she loved dearly, dying from tuberculosis at too early an age … But it is only in my later years that I came to understand her, and came to bewail my own angers against her strictness, and the way she had set up her faith as a fortress about her. My fault, my fault entirely.

I watched her, once, when the snows and ice had hit Achill Island and she had to make her way, walking, down to the girls' school where she was teacher. She picked her way through the morning, stepping like a high-stilted bird astonished across its frozen lake. We children watched, all afternoon, the disconcerting coming down of snow; as we gazed out through the window, our faces seemed to sway at times, like ghosts looking in at us from another world. And I thought of this that day, so many years later, I came to the hospital in Wexford where she was dying. Her mind was astray, now, and Father was there, nonplussed, but strong. Mother sat on the edge of the bed, her feet dangling. I wondered where, in her mind, she was now living. I searched her face for traces of her real, her actual life, but her eyes were glazed, her lips pursed. There was snow and frost on the earth when she died; the fields and hedgerows were like sheets drawn up on the newly dead. We lit tall candles about her cot. The funeral procession back to Bunclody was solemn and ungainly; I still hear the slow slushing of tyres over a bridge, the procession of cars that turned with the turns of the river Slaney, as if we formed black ribbons that bound the earth together.

For in the photograph, Mary Jo is sitting, abstracted, a 1930s beauty on her like a dream. This is the black and white of youth, I imagine the sports, the fashions, the winter slopes, and the certainties in her life that had not yet degenerated into hope. I know she would have come to this spot on a ship, festively clothed, she would have loved the movement, the companionship, the sophistication of the cruise. In the photo she is sitting at a table, the caption reads: a café near Pompeii; she is young, immortal, virginal, she lifts her glass, elated, towards the future.

And now, after the death, after my awareness of all that she had to put up with in her life, after the dreadful struggles she made to cope with her errant, alcoholic, but loving husband, I think of their love. And again there is a photograph, Don and Jo-Jo walking together, in early old age, on the beach in Keel, Achill Island. There is a sense that they are still only starting out on a pilgrimage, stepping blithely out over the gunwale of a boat, hoping to waltz on water; for love is hands, working inside one another's lives, grasping the heart, for hold. I used to hear their voices through the bedroom wall, like summer murmuring. In the good days he would bring her honeycombs in wooden frames soft as the host; and she loved him then, his shy gentleness, his own inner hurt a pitiful thing. But in the photograph they are still striding out together along the beach, they are smiling, confident, striding into the confusion of their final months, their love a bonding still, dulled perhaps, and unspoken, but for me I know they will disappear, exemplary, together, as if the sea had swallowed them, and they will leave echoes in me of a low, ongoing music.


*Teacher*

High partitions folding on themselves,
chalkdust on the air – she was exultant,
treadling a multi-coloured globe before them,
realms of gold, voyages of discovery,
illuminated bible histories. She came home

to soda bread baking, and steeped clothes;
the butcher slaughtering his own sheep
and hauling meat in the wicker basket of his bike;
the postman stitching house to house with words,
and tourists' cars passing the gate

like half-recognised celebrities.
Achill Island, the grinding of ocean against shore,
sheep shrugging out shelters against the cold;
houses with sea-shell patterns on the walls
and dogs howling against an intruding moon.

God was an island elder, presiding
where small boats launched on the Atlantic
in hope of the soft white flesh of fish.
In her bright room she was exultant
and treadled a multi-coloured globe before them.

It is only in recent years that I have recognised how much Mother had to suffer in her lifetime, how much her patience and her faith must have been taxed. She developed ways of coping with it all that I could only see, at the time, as negative, as condemnatory of the world's ways if they were not in exact conformity with the rules of her faith and of her Church. It was this sense of negativity and condemnation that alienated me, unfairly, from her, though I hope I never gave her too much sorrow and rarely opposed her in her wishes. But after my early adolescence and early manhood, I did not live with her and Father, so there was more opportunity to escape from her approach to life when it threatened arguments or fights. Long after her death I began to try and come to terms with my unfair dismissal of her troubles. I was born on the 8th of December, in the year 1943. On the 8th of December, 2006, I drove from Dublin, with my wife Ursula, down to Bunclody in Co. Wexford, where she, Jo-Jo and my Father, Don, lie buried.

8th December; the day dawns dark, a slow
rain drawling across the suburbs; one bedraggled dog
chaws at something out of a spilled bin; wind-tortured leaves
blow wet against a litter-spattered wall.

News on the radio, wars, aggression, the old
indomitable hatreds; 'Lord,' she would quote,
'you are hard on mothers ...'

We set out from Cypress Downs, in a suburb of Dublin where arrogant
magpies clack at the cats below them, where only a winter-flowering
cherry was spilling blossoms over a garden wall. In the chill air, fumes
from the car were hanging, like grey clouds. Mother was very much on
my mind, with a sense of guilt that I had needlessly hurt her while she
was alive. Now, there was no way for me to get through to her, nor her to
me. Or perhaps, there was ...?

8th December, I hear it again, that scream of pain
forced from a proud woman; a midwife
(eager for fags and a rutted lane towards home)
stepping on stone-tiled floors with a tsk-tsk sharpness,
holds basin, linen, the instruments of her art. Such
an inconceivable moment, and I am intimately
involved. Grey day, and cold, with the fire
of a suffering beyond my comprehension. For which,
mother, these thanks, these
                                        decades late, these my pleas
for your forgiveness. Irish Catholic mother, fortress
besieged, Tower of Ivory, House of Gold ...

8 December is, of course, and always has been, a Church feast day, and it
had always been a holiday from school, and in secondary school always
a 'play-day' with better food, with the freedom to visit Limerick city and
see a picture, a film. The word immaculate was a word that was
important to Mother, the 'Immaculate Conception' being the celebration
on my birthday, and naturally it, as a doctrine, a teaching, had often
puzzled me. But I always appreciated the feast, the freedom, the day off.
Now it was a dark morning, grey daylight, this winter softened by advent
calendars and cards, people congregating at shopping centres, how many
days to Christmas? At the start of the journey we paused, too, to gather
nourishment, the *Irish Times*, bars of chocolate, three perfect pink
hyacinths in a white ceramic pot.

We headed south, towards the low hills; Ursula reading aloud this morning's office, the psalms, the antiphons and aspirations. The road above the city had a winter clarity, the Wicklow hills redeeming field, hedgerow and pasture; trees standing, a spray of mud coating their trunks, for this is quarry road, with trucks hauling away the innards from the lumpen hills, pressing muck into the tarmac, a misting of muck everywhere. From branches of a diseased elm a crow, in black cassock, grey soutane, was preaching though in high dudgeon, to the world. If it was Father who had come out with me into the winter night, who had climbed the quarry hill to watch the stars, an icy breathing of island darkness holding us about, yet it was she, perhaps, was held indoors by indoor things, oven concerns, and bucket suds; son to father, cherishing, to mother distant and different, in a dim and dimming otherness. Over a clutch of dung a whorl of dancing flies turned in regulated chaos like a universe of stars. We watched the movements of hard-hat men – a sort of Homeric statement of yellow overalls, of warrior boots – the revving-up of trucks, inexorable whittling at the core of earth for the next crude gobbets of wealth. They were big men, big-chested, certain of what they are about. And I, a little uncertain, always, of what I was about.

Madonna. Miriam. Mary of Nazareth.
There are those more beautiful
who pass like caravans on a near horizon
laden with gold out of Egypt and Ophir; she
snub-nosed, brown-skinned and undernourished, wears a few
beads of coloured glass, speaks unlovely dialect;
there are homes more beautiful, porticoes
for the moderately-off, and mansion keeps
of granite stone and marble step, cool chambers; hers

a mud-brick two-roomed shape, crowded
with family, and the lower spaces shelter sheep; hers
a brushwood roof where she can sleep at night
under the silent tumultuous stars;
she weaves, prepares and grinds, she herds,
she is a drudge, hands callused and body sore;
without dowry, scarce past puberty,
and who should desire her, save the God?

71

The first town, Blessington, its long street with new offshoots into neat and manifold estates. Grey forenoon, pre-Christmas busyness, bulbs hung above the street and wavering in the slightest breeze; commerce, a focusing on Santa-lit big windows, banks festooned with winter sleighs and much-loved reindeer, people hurrying, wrapped about themselves, hasty bonhomie and compliments of the season. We drive through, watchful, pausing for the breathing of the psalms.

She would sit at the kitchen table,
copies piled on the parti-coloured frayed oil-cloth,
grandfather bustling in from sheds, and father
pacing the floor like a displaced animal; she would tell
over and over the pounds and shillings and pence,
tut at the spellings, and the dull
reiteration of the island girls' ordinary days,

their lot
housewifery or service, the slow labouring into flesh
laden with black wools and waitingness, or their lot
exile, housewifery or service, their arms akimbo over full
breasts, hurrying into memories, nostalgia, waitingness ...

and she loved them, their staring eyes, the wool
socks inside black boots, the patchwork skirts
and cardigans, and would hymn a strict
heaven before them, a catechism of purity and care,
with tiny versicles of miracle, the sun
glancing off mauve hillside heathers onto the painted
classroom walls – till she sat back at the table, and sighed,

the pencil paused from its ticking, light fading.

Something
hydrangea-like about her, mop-head, lace-cap,
how it flourished with extravagance under a kindly sun
and hung its head all brown and frowsty against the soils
of winter; and she hoarded
sorrow at her base till it grew a virtue in her, weaponry
to hurl sorrows back against a wounding world;
Madonna. Mother. Mary Jo.

We drove, then, between low humped hills, a curved valley and, on the right, the small and laggard stream that will become the Slaney. And it was here I watched Father's eager stalking of the river's pools, and how – after such years of difficulties, a man cleaves to a woman, she to him, down all the bright dark days of their togetherness. And I tune to the radio – it is Vivaldi, the music such sweet bitterness, *nulla in mundo pax sincera.*

> In Nazareth she is not dressed in satins, nor sitting idle
> at a prie-dieu; the messenger, when he comes, comes
> like a fox, magister of the subtlest arts
> of being. Miriam was small, robust and muscular,
> she sat in the dooryard, plucking chickens, the smaller
> feathers irritating fingers, her smock
> spattered with blood after the killing; from the far
> end of the yard a goat's laughter and nearer
> the pharaoh strutting of a cock; but her dark eyes
> watched beyond the hen-shit, if she could not read
> nor write, she held the history of the tribes
> vividly in memory, could see past the blood
> > of Nahum, Samson, Abel
> into the hurt and tender eyes of God; hers
> an unremarkable graced dailiness, though why the Spirit
> should fall on her out of the chaos she did not
> understand, she did not understand.

As I drove, the river now on our right, a slight rain falling outside, misting the windows, drawing a peace-filled silence between Ursula and me, I remembered those times Mother had deeply moved me. I remembered the big bedroom, Achill, she sitting before the dressing-table, her favourite tortoise-shell-framed hand-mirror before her face; at that moment there was something in the stillness moved me, while she was watching far beyond, out the big window across bogland towards the distant sound, unmoving, though her lifted hand was trembling slightly; now I knew how the souls of those who have passed come smiling across an inner vision that strikes us numb, at times, though restless: witnesses, to assoil the living, on the trail the dead have passed along, and cautioning. She shivered, suddenly, laughed towards me and said: I think somebody has walked across my grave.

Nazareth, evening. After one day's mongering and dole
he stands to ponder the life of a man, a Jew-boy, this day's
exorbitant samenesses, all the days like peels
of white wood curling in the corner of a yard;
by the lake the woman, Jew-girl, scarce past puberty,
has spread linens out over scorched grass, stands
in the shade of a tree, dreaming: of a Jew-boy, a house;
she turns, there in the gentle emptiness of the day,
laying her tunic down, moving her dark-brown body gratefully
into the water; beautiful the movements, her hands
piling the grape-black hair at her nape, bone of her spine
enchanting as she wades in water till she stands,
waves lapping her breasts, the rose evening
breathlessly still, as he is, watching.

She turns and her small breasts are firm
in the fading light, the flower of her navel,
the darkening delta of her maidenhair and her thighs
rising out of the water, the water
tiny golden gifts against her skin;
she stands, unabashed, a while, her hands
gentle against the stomach-flesh, and he stands,
watching; she dresses, still wet, lightened
by her bathing and he hears her voice, a soft
and animal laughter as she moves along the shore
to stand in quiet praise and be a part of it,
the dark of early night, the trees, the water.
Out in the yard tonight they will tell
tall stories, they will sing sad songs
to the night-birds, to the kindly stars; he
will be silent, hushed in himself, and wondering.

Jo-Jo is sitting on a rug, hugging herself small inside the wind; they are all on the beach, near the great Cathedral cliffs; but she is beyond the fray of family. Withdrawn. Self-conscious. Offshore, the waves swell impetuously and break as a line of foam goes racing angularly across the crests, the break and long-flow reaching in along the beach. She has been reading a murder mystery, but something – voice or gull or sudden catch of sorrow – has her pause, and hold the book against her breast to watch inwards; the beauty, the enormity of the Atlantic won't touch her there; her ganglion of nerves, of bone and flesh and tissue holds a moment out of the impetus as she penetrates, despite herself, the dreadful wall that lifts always against our littleness. I see her shudder, her eyes recover the wild light of sea and she returns, gratefully, to the artificial mystery.

> As an orchid among buttercups is she, as a peach tree
> among brambles in the wood; as exile
> in a hostile land, as drudge among the very poor.
> Sometimes the soul, swollen with the news of creation,
> grows too great for the body and leads it forth
> on a journey, over fruitless hillsides, across stone-ridden
> uplands, in an outflow of praise and wonder. Hers, yet,
> a long apprenticeship to pain, before she grows
> mistress of it, and settles down to the long night.

Left now, at the filling station; we have been down this road before, several times. Mine is a raid on memory, the needed booty – forgiveness; how we misunderstand each other, wilfully sometimes, more usually out of ignorance and conceit. Suddenly a rabbit, colour of milked tea but with white ankle-socks and a Christ-child scut of the purest white; a nibbler, big-bidder, delicate on the scutch-tips, and wary. He skipped quickly off the road, through a gap somewhere in the ditch, and disappeared. We passed the wayside grotto, Madonna, lime-white and blue-gloss, having little to do with our passing, this stylised, bathetic woman, not mother, a place to burn small lights, ushering prayers away in streels of smoke. These lowroads, twisting to the ancient laying-out of fields, dull, untaxing.

> Miriam moved, unnoticed, among many
> in the caravansary, road-weary, wearied too
> by the not-to-be-admitted knowledge; slept
> with the animals, their warmth, their comfortable

snores and shufflings in the dark;
the camel drivers were speaking quietly together
the world's gossip, and how the tetrarch
was building palaces to himself; the muleteers
in the other yard talked drunkenly, farted, argued;
games of dice, the stench of sweat and greed;

until she slipped away, beyond the dawn, into
cinnamon-coloured hills, a merlin
circling round its cry and tiny furred and frightened lives
busy amongst the rocks and scrub. The world
                    troubled, and everywhere the powerful
fattening on detritus of rioting and wars. And sat, stilled,
small and invisible on a parched slope, in need
of woman-talk and sustenance, scared of the journey done,
more scared of the journey yet to come.

Here is a man whose dreams bear fruit. And here
is Nazareth, a village without importance, and Aramaic,
a language of strange utterance; here is Miriam, betrothed,
a girl of no importance, poor, unlearned, menial, drudge.
Here is a man, Torah-observing Jew, big-handed,
scarcely-worded carpenter, and the angels visit him
in his dreams. In cases like these, they tell us, marriage
comes first and love, perhaps, comes later.

        My soul extols the greatness of the Lord
and my spirit exults in God who saves me,
for he has heeded and loved the lowliness of his servant.
And see, from this day out every generation shall know me blest,
for the mightiest One has worked wonderful things for me
                                and holy is his name.
Down all the generations his mercy swells to those
        who love him.
And in this way the strength of God has been made manifest:
the arrogant in the hardness of their heart
        have been strewn about,
and the powerful pulled from their thrones, our God
has lifted up on high those who had been degraded;

he has fed the hungry full with the best of gifts
and those who are rich have been banished empty from his sight.
Remembering the greatness of his mercy
he has come to the aid of the oppressed,
for this has been his promise from the distant past
and will be kept down all the centuries to come.

I was sent in with messages; there was a hum from the two-roomed schoolhouse, her fiefdom; without democracy, for its own good; here she stood, mistress, the word mother would not apply. In the small hallway there was a smell of cocoa and damp coats; for me the embarrassment of girls, their smirks, their implausible and whispered comments. A sudden silence as I moved across to her desk, chalk-marks on the blackboard, the whole puzzle being elucidated in one of its smaller parts; and now? after decades; the school became a woodwork shop, it became, after failure, an abandoned husk, small dunes of wood-dust, shavings, something banging in the breeze with mild-mannered impatience, and only persistent island winds that come fingering grass and nettle, rust-work, and love, long missed.

They had gone on beyond the city, her pains
causing her to cry out at times and he, hurt
and ignorant and distraught, led the reluctant ass
towards the shelter of hills; a low, blue-black sky,
stars sharp already as nails, a chill wind blowing.
He would lay her down among the scrub, if necessary,
the donkey-blanket beneath her, water from a stream
to help the cleansing; there would be night-birds,
jackals, perhaps, and snakes. The great howl of the ass
frightened him and he held the woman tightly
against the cruelties of shale and the unshareable pangs
of a full pregnancy. Till the gathering dark
drew them to a small fire; in the limestone hills
a cave, small shelter against the winds, and crude
half-drunk shepherds gobbing at a fire; they heard
small life-sounds, the shiftings of a flock
and she cried again, as the lost do, against the pain.

We came out, then, on the main road, between Carlow and Enniscorthy;
I eased my grip on the wheel; a truck sent up a spray of dirtied rain as
we sped past. I was thinking how much I love the woman quiet beside
me on this searing trip. Mount Leinster invisible in the gathered mists,
this rich-soil land fallow and puddled in the Irish winter. Slaney broader
now, its dark flow soiled with a factory's olive outspill, and trees being
hacked out of the way for some no-doubt necessary building. I reached,
touching the woman's hand, for presence, reassurance, warmth.

> Walnuts, figs; the tiniest hairs of the gooseberry;
> she would touch the sap of balsam trees
> to her children's skin, cure headache and weeping eyes;
> she would rub docken leaves where the sting of nettles
> scalded. Morning, the jacaranda tree letting go
> its misty dreaming, it could be again the outset of the world
> where man and animal stand astonished. Under
>     the dreeping bush
> she sets out, deep-breathing, to take her place before the class;
> her children brought to task, the strange one
> hungry at the carpenter's desk; there is poverty, taxation, a little
> beggary, and at times her own unruly sons
> pestering the neighbours; she prepares a barley porridge,
> for supper there will be cucumbers, onions, nuts and oranges;
> on each fourth Sabbath, a salted fish; potato bread and farl,
> cabbage cooked in bacon stock, thick and smoked rasher slices;
> on Fridays herring, in Lent one meal and two collations.

And then we were slowing down the long hill into Bunclody; a varied
shrubbery, the small town laying itself out below; a soft-toned town, to
retire to. Don and Jo-Jo had come here, to spend their later years away
from the city, in a quiet where they could cultivate the garden, read, be
calm and loving together, without the distress of needy children, the
demands of earning a living. I ease the car to a halt, opposite the
bungalow, memories like exhaust fumes stirring through the heavy air;
there the plants he nursed, soil he laboured; that window was her room,
her privacy, her prayer-time, ministries; blank now, reflecting this bleak
day, and unresponding. After her death, the house loud with visitors, I

slept alone in her room and in her bed; the moon sent a dull, pre-Christmas light through the curtains; I knew, at last, a weight of sadness, a slow welling of loss; a scent remained, her talcs and creams, the dressing-table things, a glass tea-tray for rings and hairpins, and there in the empty hours after dawn, I saw her tortoise-shell hand-mirror, dusted, and a crinkled prayer-card to St Anthony, patron of all lost things. Mother. Who has taken away with her bundles of sufferings, inflated anxieties for her children's souls, and every possibility of mutual understanding and forgiveness.

On then, the river again on our left, through the rich and fallow fields, till we drew up, at last, by the graveyard wall under dripping trees. That certain pause, a small silence, and then the gathering of coats, umbrellas, the pot with its three pink hyacinths. The car doors closed, startling through the almost stillness of the rain, intrusive ping-song of the automatic lock, and then, destination, the rising recurrent sorrow of the merely human before loss, its unacceptability, its disdain.

After it all, after all this, the years, the distances, after the days and absences and angers, what can I do but stand in stillness by the grave, her name and his, only a dream breeze touching the trees and a soft rain falling. Stand, nothing to say, all said, winter, and grey, my presence I hope amounting to something, to sorrow, pleading, the three pink hyacinths. I step across her grave to lay them by the headstone, offering a presence more eloquent than mine. And I think of the distant Mother, and her child, the light along the body is olive green; I wonder if they would have draped him across her knees? the blood, the gore, the fluids. I wonder if she even had that much comfort? This loved and cared-for body torn now, reviled; that she bore and birthed in anxiety and sorrow; God's abandonment of him is doubly hers. And can you hear them all, the women? mothers, daughters, sisters … their cries across time and space, joining with her in ongoing silence that shatters the world across every century, crying against war and killing, against crucifixion, torture, rape, the fact of the disappeared, the pulling down of love.

## Miscellany: The Scholar

⁂

Dear Mother: (I write to her from the Burns library: but the words of the letter remain in my mind, only) There have been days of rain here in Boston, this late winter. It comes as a surprise to me who prepared long and hard for snow, and frost and ice. I am brought back out of the unfamiliar to days I had thought long faded out of memory and have been smitten again by the vagaries of the mind. Do you remember those long rainy days we would sit inside and watch through half-fogged windows, boredom holding us, tired of the books? Oh yes, you were bustling about, forever busy, a lot of it unnecessary, passing the time, I think, as if time were a threat and not something that would run out for you, as it will for me, sometime, and who knows when? Things here are strange, familiar too. Small hard banks of snow remain and no, there's no sign yet of spring. I remember how excited you used to be as the buds appeared, as if suddenly, on the fuchsia hedge. Here the winter holds, it has longer arms, winds stretching down over Canada with thin and chilling fingertips. I remember that story of the Snow Queen you used to read to me, well over half a century ago, I was stirred by the tale of ice lodged in the eye and heart, throwing a different view of love about the world, where the Snow Queen ruled in her palace of ice, where the northern lights, the aurora borealis, were a kind of chill and lovely firework display.

And then there are the birds, or not. During the snowstorm that came through like a vast, rushing express train some weeks ago, all the birds seemed to have disappeared, as if they had caught that train and moved on south. There was an eerie silence in the garden, and among the trees by Boston College a dreary absence. I heard a chuckling sound one day and saw a congregation of sparrows in under the shelter of a bush where the snow had never reached; they were setting up a rumpus, a debate, no doubt, on weather but all of them were chattering at once and not a word of sense amongst them. I stopped and watched, feeling, well, here are familiar creatures, behaving as they did when you and I stood out one winter and flung them tiny moistened crumbs of bread. You must remember? How we shooed the eager cat away indoors? And when that bully magpie came, scolding and threatening from the garden wall, how you took pity on it, too, aren't they all God's little creatures, you said.

Isn't it strange how you may be walking down miles-long Commonwealth Avenue and all that you can think about is the backyard of home, the blue-black apron of your mother speckled with the tiniest of daisies, and the squabbling of house-sparrows, familiar as the old rusty gate you swung on? *Anseo*, Mother, here I am. Then today, along the rain, there came a kind of clearance, that work of sunshine to get through and you can sense a glow in the world, a light that sings already deep in the heart, like the promise of lilac back into the world. And there he was, the cardinal bird, perky red crest and aggressive red beak, there in flesh and feather, a brilliant red with a black bib that takes nothing away from his preening glory. I took his coming, as a welcome to this stranger from the west of Ireland, a loud 'halloo' as if to say 'Now just you wait, all this dull, damp city of Boston will clarify itself, and will become a playground filled with sunshine and good cheer.' And there, right beyond the cardinal, the catbird, oh yes I had heard of him, grey and secretive, but with that strange and haunting cry like the mewing of a sorry cat, and he called out, that sharp-shriek mewling sound and all I could think of was your phrase, little boys should be seen and not heard. And here I am, *Anseo*, talking to you, and you have been gone now a quarter of a century. Something about the heart, and its ongoing will to lift into bright skies of hope and love, something about walking here, in a strange city, growing aware of a love that was offered to me so many years before I grew aware of it, and relished it. Thank you, Mother. Thank you.

*Two*

*Down the Long Corridors*

჻

It had begun in an island innocence.

It had continued in unquestioned and unquestioning belief.

It began again in a grey, huge building, standing far back from the city, Limerick; it began again far back from the country road, and utterly far from the island. It was on a hill, behind a long row of sycamores. Mungret Village, two miles or so up the road. Mungret College, run by the Jesuits; a boarding school. Secondary school. Islanded from happiness. On either side of the long lane up to the building were fields, great meadows and trampled pasturelands. Beyond the building were playing fields, the high white poles of goalposts, the hanging nets of tennis courts. There were overwhelmingly long corridors, staircases, dormitories, classrooms. It was a loss of intimacy, a loss of privacy. There was a terrible sense, too, of loneliness, even though my elder brother, Declan, had been already two years here and knew how to negotiate the ways and worries. There was a large, barn-like refectory where I bundled in, silenced and in shock, with many others, as new and as small and as cowed as I was. I shrank and crept about as quietly as I could until I was shown through a long dormitory with separate cells divided by wooden partitions, into a smaller room where there were a dozen beds, without partitions.

The windows were high and large and curtainless. Uncertain September light kept the dormitory bathed in a faint glow, from moon, or stars, I did not know. I heard shuffling and stirring from the others around me; I thought I heard sighs, and someone sobbing. Gradually the night darkened, gradually I began to doze. I slept, but the sleep was restless and I dreamt I was climbing through tunnels of trees and into sea-caves where everything was dark, where threatening figures loomed out of the branches and reached down from the dripping roofs. I tried to cry out, for help, but my throat would not sound. And then something enormous, black and white, like a bear, came crashing loudly through the fuchsia and rhododendron tunnels and a great black paw, the claws sharp and extended, began to reach for me.

I woke, suddenly. I was sweating. I felt cruelly at a loss when I woke. I was sitting on a hard, wooden floor, somewhere. I was in my pyjamas but I had a thin eiderdown wrapped about my body. I was leaning back against a wall and a pale light glimmered in on me from a high window. I found, too, that I was crying, softly, to myself. For a while I believed I was still in some strange dream; I had no idea where I was, nor even who I was. Only gradually did awareness return; I was frightened and astonished to find myself in a large dormitory, with the separate cubicles, all of them with their curtains drawn across the entrances. I was at the other end of the college from my own small dormitory and I had no idea, except that I had walked in my sleep, how I had come there.

For a moment, after I stood up, I felt like shouting for help. I stopped myself, in time. Perhaps, I thought, I had somehow come in search of Declan, who would be sleeping in a proper dormitory. I gathered the eiderdown around my shivering body and tried to gauge the direction back to my own bed. Judging by the light of the quarter moon that was low on the sky, I began to move, very slowly, holding my body against the wall. When the darkness fell completely as a cloud came across the moon, I groped along with one hand in front of me, my body gliding against the wall. Eventually I reached another wall that came out at right angles; I turned along with the new wall and continued to move. I came to an opening. I paused. I had no idea if I was right or not. I waited. Soon the moon came out again, shedding the smallest light but sufficient to show me that I was back at the archway into the small dormitory. With enormous relief I moved, quickly now, back into my own bed and lay down.

I was very cold, and very frightened. I felt, right now, that I might not be able to last long in this place. It was a world too different to the world I knew. And everything was alien to me, I had never felt so alone in my life. Around me I could hear some of the others, restless too in their sleep. One of the boys was whimpering, softly, like a kitten lost under floorboards. It was, strangely, a comfort to me; at least I was not the only one disturbed by the night, the difference, the unknown. I sat up for a moment and reached to the small locker beside my bed; I had left my fob watch in such a way that I might be able to read the time from my bed, but it was too dark. I took the watch and tried to read it under the faintest of light still coming through the window but it was no good. I listened for a short while to the gentle ticking of the watch, then I left it back on the locker. Soon, I slept again, a deep, blank sleep, scarcely moving until the sudden shrill scream of the electric bell ripped me out of the bed into a dark morning, into another, unwelcome morning. My ordeal in secondary, boarding school, had begun.

That first class day began with Latin. In a classroom that was called Elements, I found myself among some thirty other boys. Each of us carried a bundle of books balanced on a thick slate. We placed the books on the desks before us. We waited. I was sitting towards the back, at the wall. Beside me was a plump boy still dressed in short trousers. I was glad of my own good clothes now, and proud of my shirt, my jacket and my college tie. I felt, for a moment, that this might yet be all right. I nodded at the plump boy and then glanced around at the rest of the class. They were all nervous and timid, touching their books, opening them desultorily, waiting.

Fr MacShane was a big man. He was a Jesuit. He came sweeping into the classroom, his long black gown like a trail of angry wind behind him.

'Stand up, all of you, when I come into the classroom!' he shouted.

The boys stood, terrified. Fr MacShane said a few quick prayers and the boys murmured 'Amen'. The priest slammed down some books on his desk and turned back to the class. 'Sit!' he ordered, and we sat. This was going to be difficult; I tried to cower even more into my seat, to hide. Fr MacShane moved menacingly back and forth at the head of the class. He had fair hair, neatly arranged over a big, intent face, great bushy eyebrows shading sparkling grey eyes, freckles on the round face and a nose that was too large and suffering from tiny perforations.

'Latin!' he bellowed. 'We are going to begin Latin. You will love it. It is easy. This class is called Elements, Elements so it is, and we are only beginning. If you follow willingly and intelligently you will come with me into a great world of classical wonder and linguistic magic that will open up the whole of Europe to you, Europe, its history, its languages, French, Spanish, Italian, and on even into the bad English that you speak. It is the language of the Church, is Latin, so it is, and therefore it is a holy language and therefore this class is a sacred place and you are going to live in the blessed comfort of the Church. Are you with me, boys, are you with me?'

There was silence. Yet something had already stirred in my soul, some excitement I could scarcely comprehend. I could see the small and muddied stream that ran alongside the road before our house on the island, I could hear the cries of hungry sheep in the small fields and the howling of the winds in off the Atlantic through the scrawny and arthritic limbs of the thorn bushes. I remembered how the mysteries of the Latin I had learned for responses to the Mass had intrigued me with their music and difference. And already this priest, this frightening, large man, had opened up intriguing corridors that he said would lead us into worlds of magic and wonder.

'Right!' said Fr MacShane sarcastically. 'I see we have a bunch of linguists here, linguists who do not know how to speak! But on we go, on we go, we'll see, boys, we'll see. Open up your book, your Latin grammar book and let us make a start. Page one, chapter one, the verb, to be. *Sum, es, est, sumus, estis, sunt ...*'

'Whatever you bind on earth shall be bound in heaven,' the Rudiments religion teacher was saying. I had moved on, from Elements into Rudiments, and was getting to know the way around this Jesuit college. It was less than three months since I had grasped the delight of learning new and exciting stuff. I was doing very well, academically, my heart straining for acknowledgement, my spirit seeking reassurance. 'So now, who makes these laws? and what right have they to make these laws, binding and loosing on earth and in heaven? Eh? who has the power to make such laws?'

There was a long silence. The priest glared about the class. Fr O'Shea was small and vole-like, his nose long and sharp, hairs peering out of that nose, long loose strands of hair drawn across a bald skull. I had taken a dislike to the man, though I did not yet know him. 'Jacko,' he was called, and he held his class taut in expectation of punishment and sarcasm.

'Nice to know,' Fr O'Shea went on, 'what a fine bunch of saints and scholars we have in this class. Oh yes, saints. Look at ye! Sheep and goats! Catholics, indeed! Idiots, more like. You, boy, from the island!' I was startled, Fr O'Shea was looking straight at me. 'Yes, you, you, the boy with seaweed in his ears, what?'

The other boys in the classroom snickered.

'Name some of the laws of the Church, boy.'

'We have to go to Mass on a Sunday, Father.'

'Good, good, Mr Deane, well done! Mass on Sunday, yes. Only on Sunday, eh?'

'On holidays of obligation Father.'

Jacko was getting no pleasure from this encounter. He paused, then pounced on another boy.

'Name one of those, you boy, there, Mr White, isn't it?'

Jimmy White was taken aback; he had been gazing towards the window. The sun shone out in the world in a late autumn glow that reminded us all of the summer break, and of the long months ahead when the college building could be cold and the lessons tough.

'Em, one of them, Father?'

'Oh yes, I thought so. No attention to your faith, no sense of belief at all at all.'

Jacko took the boy by the ear and half dragged him out of his desk. 'One of them yes, one of them. You're certainly one of them. You are called Mr White, are you not? Have you a white brain, boy? Is it white? Or were you looking at something special out there, outside our window? Tell us, tell the class what you were smirking at.'

'Nothing, Father, I was thinking, Father, that's all, about what you were saying.'

'You were thinking, were you, Mr White? Too much effort for you, I'd say. What were you thinking about, if I may ask? Tell me what I was talking about, do.' He kept hold of the boy's ear which had turned very red under the pressure.

'Em, you were talking about the holidays, Father.'

'Good. Good. What holidays? Name some.'

There was a pause. 'The summer holidays, Father, the winter ...'

'Hah!' shouted Jacko with some satisfaction. 'I thought so. Not listening. Thinking about some girl out in the city, eh?'

'No sir, no Father.'

Jacko released the boy, went back to the teacher's desk, took up the punishment notebook and began writing out a docket for the Dean of Studies. He handed it to poor Jimmy White. Every afternoon, after classes were over, all the boys with such dockets had to report to the Dean of

Studies to receive the number of slaps written on the docket. Fr Erraught, Dean, kept a large pandy-bat in a pocket inside his soutane. The strap. Leather, stitched thick, hard, slightly flexible. Six on each hand from this large priest and the palms of the hands – sometimes, too, slipping up along the wrist – would be red, stinging, and occasionally bleeding. The priest, 'The Rat', he was called, but quietly, furtively, with a deadly hatred, appeared to relish the task, to lay his large body into it, his adult strength into the slaps. The next day, the docket, stamped, would have to be handed back to the teacher. 'Proof, boys,' Jacko went on in his acid voice. 'Proof that even if you have all the bones and the flesh and the blood in the one place at the one time, you will not necessarily have a person. Like Mr White, he's there, but he's not *here*. Ha, ha, ha!'

There was no answering snicker from the class. Religious studies had become something black and hideous, something worse than algebra or quadratic equations or subjunctives. God had become a punishment, someone to be slunk away from, someone you worked to avoid attracting his attention to you. The word 'love': *amo, amas, amat, amamus, amatis, amant* ... became an easy Latin word to conjugate, and had nothing to do with God. Nothing at all.

The years went by, slowly, painfully, and gradually I lost my sense of obedience and respect. I learned, but it was now almost against my will. I rebelled, at times, against the cold-hearted approach of the priests. I was punished, several times. The sting of the leather left my palms sore and hot for hours. Resentments grew in me and in others. And yet I had my elder brother, Declan, just ahead of me, and Declan was a model student and had announced that he wanted to join the Jesuits himself. A special and a new mode of care was transferred from the priests to the younger brother, to me. Elements and Rudiments were over; there followed the Grammar year; the final years were Syntax, Poetry and Grammar. I held on; I moved amongst the wilder boys, keeping a certain distance even from them and so I felt, at times, a desperate loneliness.

That boy, the one who had begun in bright hope and excitement, is a curious creature, rebellious in a half-hearted way, mostly, I believe, over the loss of my freedoms on Achill Island. Yet I was open, too, and not wholly spoiled. For there were things that did touch me, even though I worked to keep them at some distance from myself: there was literature, language, music, and there was faith. I had studied the piano on Achill Island and continued that study in college, so they made me one of the organists, to accompany the hymns for Mass and Benediction. I was always nervous about that but managed reasonably well. The organ was an old one, two-manual, pedals, though for a time I could not manage to work the latter, my feet, in the early years, not able to reach down far enough. The organ was wind-operated and another boy had to pump the handle, up, down, up, down, for as long as the music was played. It was quaint, wheezy, and gave rise to much fun, and an uncertain level of volume.

> He was up in the choir-loft, tuning the pipes
> of the old century's wind-pump organ; I heard
> taps and bangs on metal, strange half-throated off-
> notes, near-notes, puffs, sighs and cough-blasts;
>
> and then he was playing – Bach, Buxtehude, Brahms –
> it was a young Jehovah's making, a bright hands-full
> soaring over oceans of soul-light, filling the chill of the chapel
> with a lush of breathing. Now, in my everyday listening,
>
> for the poem, the music, I am Mary before the ash-soft fall
> of the messenger, I am John after the disappearance
> beyond the clouds. I listen to the silence beyond the thuck
> and thudding of a day's importance, to hear the hum that figures
>
> a countryside of darkness, the sounds of April
> whispering over into May, the thunder of apple blossoms
> dropping from the tree; I listen for the tune that my days make
> in the works of love, in the notes' approximations to a symphony.

Before Easter, that final year of my secondary schooling, all the boys were taken, one by one, by Fr Sheehan for a 'serious conversation'. The boys joked about it, about his seriousness, his innocence, but I knew that behind their mockery he had touched them. I felt, as my turn approached, that I must be careful, not to admit to serious doubts about God; I knew that my own worth in this school was not high, that Declan, now in the Jesuit novitiate in Emo, was the only real reason I was tolerated here. I determined to set up a wall of silent obtuseness, this small priest would not get behind it.

'Sit down, Mr Deane, sit down,' Fr Sheehan said, ushering me to an uncomfortable chair in front of an enormous desk. I sat, stiff and watchful. The priest fiddled around a little on his desk for a while, selected some papers, smiled at me, then sat in his own swivel chair on the other side of the large desk. 'Ah!' he said suddenly, smiled again, then opened a drawer in the desk. He rooted around in there, took out an already opened box of liquorice allsorts, and a brown paper bag with some other kind of sweets. 'Allsorts, or mint, Mr Deane?'

'No thanks, Father,' I said, wishing to remain unembarrassed and unselfconscious.

'Love these myself, if you'll excuse me,' Fr Sheehan said, dipping into the paper bag and taking out a few sweets wrapped in crinkly paper. He smiled again, left the sweets on the desk and closed the drawer.

'I suppose I don't have to tell you the facts of life, Mr Deane?' he began, without embarrassment, though looking sharply at me.

'No, Father, my own father ...'

'Ah yes, of course, of course. Then I'll just stick to the question of ... well the question of your following your brother Declan, a vocation, I mean? Do you follow?'

'Yes, Father.'

Fr Sheehan glanced through the notes he had in front of him, looked up once or twice and smiled. I knew there would not be much praise among those notes! I had taken part in the night-time occupation we called 'rackets', banging our zinc basins against the wooden partitions of our cubicles to create a mighty noise; all this to cause trouble, to signify our discontent, particularly with one priest, a cruel man who thwarted our sometimes (though not always) innocent escapades. I had been punished several times for taking part in such activities: punished by getting six blows from the pandy-bat on my naked backside! I accepted all of that, feeling I deserved it. And it never stopped me from finding other ways of expressing my distaste for the college and its regime. But now Fr Sheehan pushed the papers to one side. 'All quite satisfactory there, Mr Deane, most satisfactory indeed. A few high jinks, perhaps, high spirits, a good thing in the young, don't you think? Splendid! Splendid!'

The priest sat back in some satisfaction and swivelled himself a little on the chair. He joined his hands then and brought the two of them to his chin.

'And now, Mr Deane, the priesthood. The seminary, all of that. How do you feel, is there any stirring in you that might announce a vocation? Any stirring at all?'

There was an innocence and openness about Fr Sheehan that I found hard to resist.

'I'm not sure, Father,' I began, in spite of all my watchfulness. I felt, now, it might not be fair to pretend. 'I've been troubled. I've had doubts. And I know that I am very happy when I'm at home, when I'm in the world, like. There's so much …'

'Ah yes, I see, I see, the world, the flesh … yes, yes, all of that, all of that. I understand, of course.'

'It's all so beautiful out there, Father, I mean, there's the world of nature itself, the trees, the sea, the mountains, all that freedom, and there's things like music and travel and all of that, things a priest could not do, and there's, em, there's …'

'There are women, Mr Deane, girls, and family, and love. All of that, yes, yes of course. All of that. It comes down to what we want out of life, son, I mean, in the end it comes down to what we have done, what we have achieved. Cars and houses and journeys are all wonderful, don't get me wrong, and family, love and all of that, quite perfect and holy and wonderful. It's a question, son, of desire. Do you follow? Will we ever find satisfaction for our desires, that's the question. It comes down to that, what we long for in our lives, what we see as our heart's desire. Let me tell you a little story, if I may.'

Fr Sheehan leaned forward and laid his elbows on the desk before him, his hands still joined, as if in prayer, on the desk. He looked at me for a moment. 'I am going to tell you about my father, my own father. You will be kind enough, I know it, I know it, not to pass along any of this to your friends, it's private, between you and me. OK?'

'Of course, Father, of course.'

'My father was a fisherman, I don't mean professional, I mean he fished for pleasure. In the river Blackwater that flowed not far from our home. His great urge was to fish, his longing to spend as much time as he could on the banks of the river, or sometimes wading out into the flow, fly-fishing. I don't know if you've ever done that, Jackie – I may call you that, for the moment, seeing as how we are trading confidences – but it is a fascinating and a specialist pleasure. I used to watch him, when he came home from work of an evening, on those calm evenings, and I could see at once that he was almost overcome with longing, to be out there, fishing. And I would watch the prelude to his great plans, the laying-out on the kitchen table of the artificial flies he kept in a leather-wallet pouch.

It was folded over and over and he would stretch it out, exposing all the range of flies that he had. He would look out at the evening, the light, whether the alders were bending with the wind or just whispering to themselves, and then he would bend down over that pouch with complete attention, choosing the perfect lure for that evening. I remember the names of some of them, great names like *attractor nymphs, the blue-winged olive, the cinnamon sedge, the thunder bug*. Can you imagine it, Jackie, a small artificial fly called *thunder bug*?' The priest laughed quietly, and I responded. My hands were sweating a little, I rubbed them secretly against my trousers.

'And some of them, their colours, the hairs or feathers or whatever they were, some of them were really beautiful, beautiful as anything in the world could be. There was turquoise, fawn-gold, emerald, bright orange, and all sorts of stripes and streaks and tails, like miniature peacocks. But what always hurt me, Jackie, always, were the hooks, small and cruel, copper-coloured usually, and their desperate barbs were hidden and camouflaged in the beauty. You see what I'm getting at son, you surely see. He would choose, put aside the three or four for that evening. Then he would get dressed up, a special old jacket in which he stuck the flies, his rod that came in pieces that he would have to put together, carefully, oh all the preparation, the anticipation, that was the greatest part, the desire, Jackie, the desire. And the waders, pulled up over an old pair of trousers, right up as far as his waist. And I would see him move up and down the bank of the river, watching, gauging, even listening, yes I believe he was listening for the chattering of trout, and sometimes he would wade out into the water, bracing himself against the flow, he would test his wrist, flicking beautifully the almost impossible thinness of the rod and I'd admire how the light green line would curve out over his head, over the water and the fly would land, oh just so, just so. Wonderful, Jackie, wonderful. And yet, do you know, he was always uncertain, my father, something would always hurt that longing within him, some sense that this was a waste of time, that he would catch nothing, nothing, that he ought to be elsewhere, at his duties, oh something was not quite right, not like the Fisher of Men that we know and love, not like the Christ, Jackie, not like the Christ. And so often I would see him, that big body of his would droop in a kind of disappointment, a failure, even if he had caught two or three reasonably-sized trout, I would see how his eagerness would die into weariness, I would watch him restore the flies to the pouch, he was packing his longing away, for the moment, for now. And so often, as night came down I would see him walk the floor, at a loss in himself, he was like a fox, taut and watching, and I imagined and I think I sometimes heard his whispering lisping words as he prayed, for something more, something neither he nor I, nor indeed my mother, ever could put a name to. And it was that pacing to and fro on the kitchen floor that convinced me, son, convinced me utterly that I had to be certain about my own life, certain about what was important for me, certain of where I would lay my desires, so that when night comes I will not be pacing hopelessly, and wondering, Jackie, wondering …'

Fr Sheehan's words tailed off and the priest seemed to be absent a while. But the words had entered my soul where they lodged, disturbing in the weight of their quiet presence.

For I had no notion whatever of what I would do once college days had ended, once I was free again to make my own decisions, to take charge of my own life. And it was one day shortly after the final term began that the school assembled in the chapel to hear a talk from a missionary. We trooped in, restless and indifferent, glad, perhaps, to skip a class or two simply to listen to another priest coming to draw us into his life, and his vocation. When the priest came out onto the altar, we were instantly hushed in awe and expectation. He was introduced as Fr Mellett, a 'White Father', recently returned from the missions in Africa. He stood on the altar steps before us, and above us.

He was at least six feet six inches tall and built to match, built as a heavyweight wrestler for God. His habit was all white, his hair, long as that of Buffalo Bill Cody, was white; he wore a beard, white, that flowed down onto his chest and his right hand occasionally moved down along it, almost caressing it, combing it. I remember little of what he said, but his powerful voice filled the chapel with stories of his adventures in Africa, and they coloured the edges of the dull living of my college years. His were tales of tangling with witchcraft, and witch doctors, of hacking his way through jungle and dense undergrowth to find a new tribe that had never heard of the name of Jesus, of tussles with their pagan priests which he always won by Christian trickery, brandishing his false teeth before them, urging fire from his thumb by concealing a cigarette-lighter in his fist; wrestling-matches with their champions which, of course, he won. Oh yes, he had crossed God's jungle carrying God's flag. I heard his voice ring out, over and over during that talk, 'Whom shall I send? Whom shall I send?' and my poor scholar's heart trembled within me.

In that final few months of my secondary schooling, Fr Sheehan replaced our old Latin teacher and brought the beauty of language and poetry to touch my spirit, a spirit that had already been enthused, at home in Achill, by the books and literature Father had loved and shared with us; now, for the first time during my five secondary school years, I was again enthused by language and literature. Virgil's *Aeneid*, which had merely been an instrument of torture up to then, he turned into a tale of mystery, beauty and excitement. He simply read the original in Latin, as if it were a normal thing to do, then worked through it with us, bit by bit, showing us how to discover its beauty, in the language, the adventure, the wonder.

> At pater Anchises penitus conualle uirenti
> inclusas animas superumque ad lumen ituras
> lustrabat studio recolens ...

And our efforts at translation never met with mockery or complaint, but were treated as true attempts and corrected gently, Fr Sheehan explaining everything as we went along, rejoicing in the poetry of it so that we, too, rejoiced.

> Deep in a green valley Anchises, father, stood, gazing
> at the souls imprisoned there before they could rise
> into the light of the world above ...

Aeneas' relationship with his father moved me deeply, and the incursion of the son into Hades in search of his dead father, stirred my imagination the way my own father's reading to us from Pushkin and Gogol had so often stirred me beyond the banality of my days. In spite of my denials, literature had again insinuated its meaningful touch into my life.

The examinations came to an end; they were long, difficult and tedious. The final examination I had to take was in the morning; in the afternoon I was free, but had to stay in the college, gather up all my belongings, and wait for the train the next day that would take me from Limerick back to Achill Island. Most of the boys had already gone home. It was a mild, dull afternoon. I was out, alone, down at the playing fields. At the furthest end there was a row of trees, marking the limits of the college grounds, marking the outermost edge of one of the several football fields where I had exhibited minimum skills at rugby, athletics and football. I felt a very strong sense of moving, through a ghostly borderland, between the past and the future, as if I was only now coming to some sort of meaningful awareness of myself as a person, with decisions to be taken that would be crucial to my very being. The goalposts stood high and solemn; the football pitches were empty; a scattering of seagulls moved desultorily in the distance; a few clouds, grey and heavy, scarcely moved overhead. I stood, very much alone, very much shaken.

It had begun in an island innocence. It had begun in unquestioned and unquestioning belief. It had begun again in a grey, huge building, standing far back from the city, far back from the country road, and utterly far from the island. It was on a hill, behind a long row of sycamores and tomorrow morning, I knew, I would be driven down that long avenue, leaving that dreaded grey building behind me forever. From where I stood, near the goalposts, the building looked harmless and abandoned in the distance. Soon I would have to make my way back inside, move through the empty corridors and dormitories, take my place at supper with perhaps three others in the refectory, all bustle, all chatter fallen into silence. There would be a feeling of freedom in a place where I had always known constraint and limitation; I would probably meet one or two of those Jesuit priests who, I felt, had made my life restricted, painful, laborious, and I would not have to pretend to any fellow-feeling. And yet, there in that vacant and grey late-afternoon, I knew myself wholly subdued, constrained in a new way, my soul struggling towards some kind of rebirth, or, as I was beginning to sense, perhaps a simple birth into responsibility and an acceptance of the demands of a still very immature adulthood.

There was no epiphany, no visionary excitement, no revelation. But there was a slow, though ineluctable determination, and I knew that I would tell my father – him in particular, as I felt a stronger sense of presence with him than with my mother – that I had decided to become a priest. I believed this would cause him some nervous reaction, that he knew my volatility, my immaturity, that as my period in secondary school had not been marked by application or, indeed, acceptable behaviour, perhaps I was trying merely to offer an apology, by taking on something that would prove my maturing now, my goodness, my will to make something of myself. But that may have been merely my own diffidence and lack of self-confidence. My mother, I felt, would have a simple pleasure in my decision. She would wholeheartedly approve.

I began to move back towards the college, bearing a new burden of certainty and a new awareness of the world, down along that rough and sandy track back towards the walls of the college, certain, too, that if I were to become a priest it would not be in the footsteps of my beloved brother Declan, I would not aim to be a Jesuit, no, it must be more active than that, I would not wish to be a teacher in a secondary school like this one, nor an academic, nor an intellectual: no, I would be a missionary, I would cross jungles carrying God's flag, I would become a White Father.

*Father to Son*
*(a reading of the Latin poem of Colman, c.800)*

If then you are suddenly anxious to see
that gentle land, the refuge that we both share,
go quickly, don't feel restrained by any plea

of mine, nor hint of nostalgia in my prayer.
Why should I blame the tedium of a mind
grown dull; love of home wins out, and who would dare

deflect a lover? If Christ could redefine
my life's span, renew the vigour of my days,
bring back the flowering of my age, rewind

time to make these white hairs black: who says
I too would not be tempted? You must ignore
in your deep longing, an old man's sluggish ways;

remember Virgil who sang how old age bore
all away, slowed the blood and cooled the veins,
wearying the body and wasting out the store

of life's strengths; nor is there any heat remains
in dried-out flesh. The distances across the sea,
the dangers of rough shores, all that terrifies and strains

my heart. Let you, Colman, not hesitate, be
valiant against the waves, keeping in your heart
the thought of another Colman who is, at least, free

to give advice! Then listen, before we part,
be not distracted by the world's pomp, which blows
away like wind, or the way vain dreams start

and die, smoke trails to vapour, the river flows
ever more swiftly out to sea. For your care
centres there; go gladly; the Almighty knows

your longing; to the one Hope of life, my prayer
that he govern the temper of the waves, that his hand
calm the winds, that he take himself the helm, bear

you safely over the abyss until you land
on that loveliest of shores. Live happy there, my boy,
grow famed for your good living throughout all Ireland.

Joy all your days, and after, everlasting joy.


*Miscellany (Tracks)*

There existed, in the late nineteenth century, and into the first half of the twentieth, a rail-line that ran along a beautifully scenic route between Westport and Achill Island in County Mayo. Now, in imagination, though the line and the stations and the trains have long been removed, I have been taking the slow steam train out of Westport, through Newport and Mulranny to Achill Sound. It is the only way I can travel this beautiful route, for today there is scarcely a trace of the old line in many parts of the journey, bridges have gone, family homes have been built on the place where the line ran, and all is lost; now there is ghost and spirit-travel only. Here and there you can see where the line once ran, by shore and mountainside, through rhododendron woods and fuchsia-lined ways, curving gracefully, easing its way into those fine old-fashioned stations.

The line was opened in 1894 and its first task was to carry the bodies of those drowned in the Clew Bay Disaster as emigrants, heading for the potato fields, the bothies, of Scotland, were lost when their boat capsized near Westport Harbour. A sad beginning, and there was to be a sad ending, some forty-plus years later when ten young working men were burned to death in their sleeping quarters, in Kirkintilloch, Scotland. They, too, were brought home along that beautiful railway track. The line was officially closed in 1934, reopened temporarily in 1936 to allow the road to be repaired, reopened to bring the bodies home. Freight trains ran until 1937. And that was that. A railway line running through some of the most beautiful countryside in the west of Ireland, and a line forever associated in our minds with tragedy, emigration and nightmare. By the time I came to consciousness even the iron rails had been taken up and there were great gaps in the line where bridges had been taken down. My journey, then, has to be dream-travelling, in imagination only, avoiding all sense of nightmare.

So, for me, the rickety toy-room carriages make it adventure, the other all-swavering souls alongside me as insubstantial as I. We pass, as we move off, slowly, enchantingly, embarrassing backyards with knickers, vests and underpants heisting themselves shamelessly into the winds. Soon, however, the alder-trees and the far Néifin mountains sing of the purity of leaf, the upland downland shivering deserts of the West, and we puff on like old gentlemen out for an evening stroll, among fields, by tree and hedgerow and garden wall, till we come rocking over the russet-rich, the sandstone cloud-high slimline viaduct into Newport. A pause then, to steam a little, to gather puff again, to face out past the dull back ends of business, green-slime ribbons dirtying old walls, all souls together refreshed on lemonade and spirits. We rock slowly out over the pool where Father in his dream-days stood fly-fishing, content and timeless, sea-trout playing tig with him, and winning.

There are hills now, low hills, part covered with the warm and purple wallpaper of heather, part rock and boulder and erratic and there are rich glimpses of ocean out to the west of us. Then, for an instant the pyramid-shaped mountain of St Patrick – emblem and reminder of our Christian early years – appears far across the bay. We are delayed on Mulranny hill, behind the gap-toothed Great Southern Hotel, for here they are taking on more water, while wallowing below us are the scattered islands of Clew Bay and the sacred mountain is clear and bright, reaching into clouds beyond. There's a sudden suspiration, like the rush of a risen breeze, of emigrants passing us by in the sibilant sorrowing of a rain shower against lush rhododendron; a soul lowers a window and the smell of the West – of rain and heather and hearthstone – sunders the heart once more.

Now we are waltzing along the quiet inlet of the sea, the waves easy here, an old trawler nodding gently in the late sunshine, a kestrel hovering against the dark-green shoulder blades of Tonragee. We creep, through alder and furze bush and tumble-down sheds, by hawthorn villages and fuchsia glades, and in the distance the island of Achill, like an animal lying at ease, while our own Slieve More is growing slowly visible and urging tears. For this is ghost-journeying, this is the longed-for resurrected essence of a past that we have prayed for so often that it might be elegant enough to redeem us, imagination ruefully setting by the negatives. And at last we glide, shunting into Achill Sound, and halt, juddering; I sit motionless, unwilling to step down out of the dream, unwilling to part from all those who have accompanied me across the roads and laneways, the twists and turns of a life, so many ghost-companions about me still, and so much loneliness.

*Three*

*Novice*

❧

I got it right, and I got it wrong. I told my father about the White Fathers. He said he knew of them, and he thought their address was Kimmage Manor, Dublin. I wrote. I got an answer from a priest of the Holy Ghost Fathers; he told me they were not the White Fathers, but similar, a missionary order, to Africa, and that he would welcome me to Kimmage Manor, show me around, have a chat, and then let me decide. And that was how I came to enter as a postulant – not of the White Fathers, also in Templeogue in Dublin – but of the Holy Ghost Fathers, whose great seminary, Kimmage Manor, was situated in Templeogue. The novitiate was in Kilshane, in County Tipperary.

❧

We drove slowly across Ireland, from Achill Island, crossing the bridge with a certain slight failing of the heart, heading for Kilshane, County Tipperary. It was a dull day, September, 1961 and I of the still tender age of eighteen, and a quite immature eighteen at that. Mother and Father in the car, grandmother – Nanna – and I, in the back. In my suitcase, a new black suit, new white shirts, a black tie, underwear, toiletries, and my misty dreams of what life might be all about, of who and what God was, and what a missionary priest's life, like Fr Mellett's, really entailed. As we drove through the town of Tipperary and out onto the road towards the little village of Bansha, the silence grew thick between us. I would be allowed a visit after Christmas. I would be allowed another before next summer.

We passed through the sleepy village of Bansha; I can remember a few hens in their leisurely picking, there by the side of the road. Our passage caused scarcely a breath of disturbing wind. A few miles on we turned in off the main road, between high pillars and undisturbed aristocratic trees. We followed, ever more slowly, a long meandering driveway through meadowland towards an island of trees. Then I saw the house for the first time: it was a mansion, elegant, almost regal, and a large conservatory rose alongside it. In front was a high portico with tall pillars, something that gave me a sudden sense of terror as the car rounded on a gravel foreshore. There were two other young men about my age, whispering with their parents, looking a little lost, standing as they and I did at the shuddering end of boyhood. We got out of the car, Nanna more silent than ever as she sensed the nervous anticipation in me. The great door opened and a priest stepped out. He was very tall and ascetic looking, his habit black, a small half-cape about his shoulders that he flipped back over his left shoulder time and again. He had a small, strained smile and he went forward to meet some of the others who were waiting. Granny held me close for a short while, in silence, at a loss, yet taut with pride and tenderness.

'Pray for me,' she whispered in my ear. 'Pray for me, Nanna,' I countered, glancing at the tall priest who was making his way towards my parents. The next few minutes are a blur; there were introductions, the priest answering cordially but with short, somewhat impatient sentences. And then we three, young men, postulants, were standing together, our small suitcases on the gravel by our feet, gathering ourselves into shape, hoping to become all Ariel, spirits, at the service of our Lord and Master. I remember how the loneliness gathered in one final, chilling wave as I watched the small red tail lights of the old Ford Prefect negotiate the driveway back down towards the main road.

⤛∾⤜

Many of these postulants already knew each other, having done their secondary schools in a Holy Ghost college, like Rockwell, Blackrock, St Mary's. But we were not permitted to group together, and that suited me.

I was the only one from my college. We were up with the early-morning bell, 5.50, to wash and shave in cold water, put on our soutane to which we were scarcely yet accustomed, tie it round with a white rope cincture – symbol of purity and promise of life-long celibacy – put about our necks the white collar – sign of our total obedience to God and to his representatives on earth – and the light-blue stock, token of our fidelity to Mary, the Immaculate Mother of God.

Matins in the chapel at 6.15, followed by contemplation, or mental prayer, when we worked hard to stay awake and focus our minds on the otherworld. Mass, and breakfast at 8 o'clock. And so into a wholly and holy regulated day, every minute pre-determined and so every minute of every day a source of grace in our obedience, our silence save for the half-hour of recreation after lunch. We said to ourselves the lesser hours of the office, Lauds, prime, terce, sext and none; we were back in chapel at 9 at night, for prayers and vespers, followed by compline, the final 'hour' that always ended with our singing of the *Salve Regina*, a tune and prayer I now associate forever with peaceful weariness and the promise of a deeply holy sleep. And always, at reading, at study, at those times when the Novice Master taught us the rules and regulations of the Holy Ghost Fathers, our ways to holiness, the way our young souls must and will give themselves into the hands of God, without reservation, without question. And all our prayers in Latin, the psalms, the holy office, the prayers. Wonderful. Easeful. Medieval.

> He came in through the top door –
> moody, mantled, Lord of our strange isle –
> and stood before the table, watching us;
> at once a shiver of guilt ran in my blood;
>
> he sat, we sat; and he began:
> *the company of men* …
> Of fixed purpose, wing-dip, swoop,
> he was a harrier, pitched high
>
> and haughty, with some disdain
> testing and troubling us,
> urging us, starlings, one from the other
> into our own untrusted loneliness;

> *each time I go out among mankind*
> *I return a lesser man ...*

Mealtimes were taken while listening to a reading, from the Lives of the Saints, from the Lives of the Founders (Claude Poullart des Places, and later Francis Libermann), the Rules and Constitutions ... and each day to a reading of the Martyrology, outlining many strange and difficult names, in Latin, of course. The mispronunciations, the efforts, the hesitations, often caused great hilarity amongst us listeners, though we tried to stay serious and calm under the watchful eye of the Master of Novices sitting alone at the high table.

Recreation was a walk outdoors after lunch, always in threes, in case of 'particular friendships' developing, something clearly dangerous in a seminary or monastery situation. Rain would keep us indoors, apart from the long once-a-week walk we took (in threes) out about the lovely and wooded foothills of the Galtee mountains. These walks were directed by one of ourselves who poured over maps before setting out, plotted our walk, the length of time it would take, when we would be back ... all such details carefully written down. We must have made a strange sight, young men in groups of three, all dressed in black suits, with blue stock and white collar, large black hat, sometimes boots, always raincoats at the ready. And often lost among the walkways of the hills and woods, returning late, and wet and very, very hungry. Once a week, too, on Saturday afternoons, we were allowed to 'tog out' and play football, Gaelic, or soccer, and these games were ferociously fought, offering a way of getting rid of our pent-up tensions and frustrations, charging into one another, knocking one another down. It was fun, and we bled, and did not count the cost.

> Exercise, he told us,
> the small, stiff muscle of holiness;
> and day after day we came
>
> in threes, through the cloister door,
> taking our places,
> black figures, pacing

the cinder track around a field,
hurrying in the chase,
wisdom always disappearing

ahead of us, and our God,
from his high vantage point,
cheering us on.


It was the music that continued to lift my spirit. For the Novice Master was also an enthusiast for the right, beautiful presentation of the Gregorian Chant and formed a choir from our group of forty-eight, teaching us, cajoling us, conducting. We learned the strange notation, how to move with fluid ease through the psalms, in Latin of course, the responses, the antiphons. The singing of Vespers and Compline, in particular, brought us into a monastic wood that was lit from within by its slow and seductive beauty. Alongside the Gregorian Chant, and particularly for the long and lingering solemn High Masses that were sung in the novitiate, and later on in the seminary, we learned, in four-part harmonies, the great motets, and sang the works of Palestrina, Bach, Pergolesi, Franck, Monteverdi ... and our spirits soared with the loveliness and the heart-wringing delicacy of the harmonies, the words, the prayers. All of it brought to birth in me a delight in sacred music, and from that a love for all classical music, a love and delight that have been of profound importance to me down all the years.

Palestrina: the flowing and lyrical beauty of his setting of Psalm 42 remains in my mind all the years since I first heard and sang it in Kilshane: *Sicut cervus desiderat ad fontes aquarum, ita desiderat anima mea ad te Deus*: As the deer longs for the fountains of water, so my soul longs for you Oh God. Slow, building to a gentle climax, a melody and harmony that together catch the very essence of yearning.

Orlando Lassus: sixteenth century Belgium, his skill in contrapuntal arrangement kept us on our toes, offering the excitement of a controlled race through his notes; yet for me, his setting of the 'Magnificat' of Mary, was the most beautiful, and we sang it several times at Vespers, evenings after days of prayer, manual labour, and deep involvement in the things of God. My soul magnifies your name O Lord because you have done wonderful things for me.

Thomas Tallis, sixteenth century, too, and English, his harmonies touched me deeply, often complex and very rich, carrying with them a weight of solemnity that I found, dressed as I was in choir in my soutane and surplice, a biretta held demurely in my hands, lifted me into something that must be close to a waking dream or even a mild form of ecstacy: *Spem in alium numquam habui praeter in te* ... Never have I placed my hope in any other than You, O God.

After the soft *noctem* of the Latin chant
we faced, till dawn, into a Great Silence;
we were a flock of isolated starlings
settling in the rich foliage of an oak;

all day a small brass crucifix lay heavily
on the pillow; I held and kissed it, then
folding my hands across my breast,
lay down again into medieval darkness.

⁂

We were taught, early on, to sing with gusto and commitment the rousing, march-tempo motto-song of the Holy Ghost Fathers:

Go ye afar, go teach all nations,
Bear witness unto Me,
On earth in every clime,
And I with you shall be
Until the end of time.

Lovely appear, over the mountains,
The feet of them that preach
And bring good news of peace.

I never asked, in those days, weeks, months, not once all that year of novitiate, who was this God to whom I was dedicating my life, my days, weeks, months and years. Who was this Christ I was following? To Whom was I to bear witness? Did I know him? I never asked, because I had accepted without question the God I had grown up with on Achill Island, in my home, in the chapel and school I attended. I prayed to Him, (always, then, with that capital H!) morning, mid-morning, noon, afternoon, mid-afternoon, evening, night, I spoke to Him, and to His Mother for the Holy Ghosts were dedicated, too, to the Immaculate Heart of Mary. I never asked because I felt sheltered, cushioned, honoured, by being obedient to every rule and tiny regulation that guided me through every minute of every day and every night, and all my actions were winning for me a great and lasting treasure in Heaven.

All of the hours of our days, all of the actions we did, the Office of the Blessed Virgin with its sacred hours, from Matins to Compline, all the vocal prayers, all the Great Silence that we entered into every evening after Compline, where not a word nor whisper was to be heard from then until after Mass the following morning, all the music, all the chants, all the motets, the Masses, the ceremonies, all, all, all of it given, handed down, learned and handled by us, novices, in an effort to make them really our own.

But they were not truly ours, not truly. We received them from others, as the way to salvation for ourselves and those who would be entrusted to our care. And behind all this given and received, there were almost two thousand years of trial and error, until the way and the words were proven, accepted, and delivered on. And never, never during my year in Kilshane as a novice, did I feel I ought to question anything, never did I sense that this was not really me, the person from Bunnacurry, Achill Island, who had slipped into this state almost by accident and certainly without much thought or awareness of what I was doing; never did I figure that I was going through a language and a mode of being that others had framed in their entirety and that I was fitting myself into, to serve a God that was not properly known to me, like a prince or king that I was serving but who lived and reigned in a country I would never visit, nor really know, in this life. In that given and received, for the moment, I found comfort, ease and direction.

111

To the side of Kilshane, the mansion, was a great conservatory and one of my functions, later in the year, was to go and talk with Br Malachy and gather flowers with which I would adorn the altar. It was a strange, exotic place to enter, the roof of glass being as high almost as the house itself, its wooden struts and beams painted white, the glass they held slightly stained a faint shade of green. There were several high trees down the centre of the conservatory, they reached and hung their heads against the roof, their leaves thick and wide and dark green. I never knew their names nor what country they came from. Some of them were offering great, almost obscene, red and purple flowers, large as pineapples. Others trailed long thin thread-like seeds that hung down in utter stillness towards the floor. There were two rows of flower beds running parallel to this central bed, two more along the walls to the side. All the beds were filled with strange and wonderful flowers, in all colours, in all sizes.

I could name very few of them; some looked like lilies, save that they were scarlet coloured and had long yellow tongues reaching out from them. Many of these tall plants offered bird-beak shapes, though they were in exotic and emphatic colours – yellows, oranges, blues. Flowers that took the shape of butterflies, or dragonflies, or birds. An almost overwhelming scent filled the conservatory but to me it was pleasant and reassuring. There was a small plashing sound, constant and soothing, and I often stood, quietened, right in the centre of the conservatory, directly under the apex of the rounded ceiling high above, by a pool where a small fountain dribbled down over water-lilies and huge, green pods. I could see some golden fish move slowly through the stems, and here and there a larger fish, carp, perhaps, though several of these had tails and fins of strange colours and intricate design.

Down at the end of the conservatory, over the door that led through into the cloisters, was a large crucifix, the body yellowish white, the head fallen on the shoulder. The nails and the blood, the dribbling pus from the thorn-crowned head, all were more realistic than I had ever seen before. I felt I could almost hear the hammering that fixed that too-sensitive body, with long nails, onto the wood, and how that sound, hammering still across the world, opened once and for always the abyss of our humanity. I knew then, for the first time that, in the fact of crucifixion, there would be no beauty in the body that hung there, that had writhed in its solitude, in its waiting, in the bleak and uplifted perpetuity of time.

Near the floor, to the side of the small door, was a tree that I took to be some kind of holly, though the large berries it bore were not red, like the blood-berries on the body hanging above, but a dark green. The leaves themselves, prickly and threatening, were green but with a core of rust, and beside the tree stood sunflowers, several of them tall as myself, but the flowers were stripped of their petals, the heads stood black and ugly and large, the stalks blackening and drooping, as a watcher might droop with sorrow before the crucified. For a short, intense moment, I felt a strange and strong stirring within me, a determination that I would do my very best, as priest, to bring about the world of peace and love that this man had suffered and died for. I would offer this Christ my whole life. It was, perhaps, a beginning of real, personal awareness. But it was a small start, and there was a long, long way to go.

> Novitiate, still as a village before the dawn.
> Hunched figures come, rummaging through our dreams.
> When the bell has called for the third time
>
> we will unhook huge shadows from the door and tie them on.
>
> We shift and sigh in choir like an avenue of trees.
> When the world stirs we will be still again,
> shivering and solitary on exposed headlands.

Morning; pre-dawn, in darkness, I rise, kneel at the side of the bed and murmur, *Laudeter Jesus Christus*; soon I move, embodied spiritan, down unlit corridors, sure of Christ, solitary, like Christ, though among peers, a scarcely understood impulse holding me, in the prescribed place, at the prescribed time. I am functioning now as bell-ringer, cock-crower, my brothers' keeper. By rule and regulation every breath I take gives glory to my God. I wear God's smell and carry on my person the darkness of my God. Matins, before the thrush or coal-tit, until night's soothing psalms of compline before owl or bat loom or squeak – I regulate, am regulated. I pray; am prayer. *In aeternum. Amen*.

I set to study you, your dealings with the Fathers, theirs with you; the frayed recital of adventures of your Don Quixote saints. I sit absorbed in a long low building, like the country dance halls where old friends are louching. All my concentration is on you; the dry black figures of the superiors move like stone statues and all is medieval, silent and obtuse. I have learned another language in which I am to speak to you and know such certainties and happiness and a many-layered security. Love is the word reiterated everywhere and I can decline it: *amor, amoris* ... my body held and cinctured, my spirit burning: *ignis fatuus*.

It was spring, and I had lived and prayed for over half a year in the shelter of the novitiate. Now the gardens lay as if oppressed, hydrangeas slumped like the raked-through grey of Nanna's hair, her shoulders stooped. I stood before the grotto, those images of suffering and the helpless reach of mourning, darkened further after a fall of rain. The path through the novitiate grounds was slippery, with black and rotted leaves, but I was out praying the Little Office, whispering lauds, *you make the winds your messengers, you lift us up on the wings of eagles*. The grounds were extensive, paths laid out carefully around the playing fields, under the trees, between the orchard, the vegetable garden, along the furthest verges of the meadows. I knew, mid-morning, the inhaled exhaled pleasures of isolation, my as-yet-child's heart open to the Spirit's breathing.

'Oh Jerusalem praise the Lord, Praise your God, oh Zion; Because he has firmed the bolts of your gates, and poured blessings on your sons within you; Who sends down snow like wool, who scatters the mists like ash; He sends his crystals forth like morsels. And who can stand before the face of his cold? ...'

I stood a moment, relishing the music of the words, happy to be here at this particular moment. I was near the sheds where the farm was and suddenly, there was Br Alphonsus, the man in charge of the farm, and he was beckoning to me from one of the sheds; soutane discarded, he stood in a dirt-smeared vest, grasping a sheep, her wool matted with mud, her hooves skittering in terror on the stone floor; 'hold her tight, lad, tight', he told me. I left my book – its delicate gilt-edged pages, the red-silk bookmarks – down, and held her, felt the body juddering, saw the amber eye widening till the Brother touched the humane killer to her skull, fired – and I knew the sudden desperate dead weight that dragged me down on top of her dreadfully still, hot, body. I lay sprawled over her a moment, astonished, my soutane in its pristine black gathering little spittings of dust and Br Alphonsus laughed at me. 'Thanks,' he said. 'You can get back to your prayers now, there's a good lad. Thanks for the help.'

I went back to the path along the sheds, but the moment had been spoiled, the day had darkened, and my own soul had known a sudden shock and chill. The words of the psalms now came to me spiritless and flat, but I read them through, a little carelessly, the abrupt and awful fall of the sheep, its suddenly extinguished life, the feel of the wool in its softness and then the leaden drop out of my hands, all of it left me weakened and lost and I felt, for the first time in that beautiful place, a bleak helplessness, an unassuaged dread.

By now, late March, early April, we were, perhaps, thirty-two young men, several of those who had arrived on the same day as I, having left the novitiate. Secretly. As one might creep out at night to meet a lover. Cautiously, down the carpeted stair. Slowly, lest the latch fall and disturb the sleepers. Or move forward in the regular daily routines, but slip out of the line of walkers as if for some special task or function. So that there is a gap in the choir stalls during meditation, Matins, Mass. Or there is an empty place at table. No farewell. No goodbye. No hint beforehand. Lest there be an unwarranted disturbance among the others. As if a criminal. A failure. A lost soul. Leaving behind inevitable – though temporary – disarray. Taking hold of the plough, and looking back. And letting go. A small fear, like a furred animal held a while in the eye of the raptor, waiting, hoping that the shadow will pass away, across the field, over the hill, and disappear.

Silence. The cherry tree was virgin-still in starlight; spring night, my young man's body juddering; I, given life, only to renounce it. I, Br John, my black soul hanging on the door, my black shoes in order by the bed. I would have laid my head in rest on the breast of Jesus, meaning *love*, I would have followed blindly each harsh and stone-rough track after Him, meaning *abandon*, I would have held always and only loneliness in my arms, and emptiness, the mind spinning in dizziness like a stunned wasp. Meaning *devotion*. Oh John, Br John, clean-shaven and intent, content these whiles in cincture, collar, stock, but in need – and this was later – of the whelming love of someone that would sweep away the reasonable into the foolishness of love.

Dear Nanna:

We have just finished singing Compline and I am in my cell. I always enjoy singing the *Salve Regina* even though everything is in Latin. My soutane is hanging on the back of the door like a great shadow. It is night now, though early. There is still light outside and it will be difficult to sleep. I have night prayers to say yet. Then, after the Great Silence, it will be Matins, out of darkness into the light of Christ. I feel sometimes like Nicodemus must have felt, sneaking into the presence of holiness. I feel, too, that I am of the salt earth of the island and speak with the salt accent of that earth. The altar tonight was crowded with golden lilies. You would have relished it. I pray for you night and day. Pray for me. I need your prayers.

> Your own
>
> Jackie

A letter, written in the dim light of my cell, written as a half-sensed protest, as a half-suffered dread. Written. Never sent. Torn up and dropped into the basket in tiny pieces, a small and faltering fall of snow.

### Treasure in Heaven

We came, novices professed, by bus to Dublin, thirty-one of us, still hopeful, still holding to the prayer. Some seventeen souls had seen a different light, or had bumped into a dark barrier wall, or had heard the voices of the world call out to them, and had left. Perhaps it was the silence of the God they had hoped to serve in the Congregation of the Holy Ghost that had discouraged them. Those of us who had held on had taken the simple vows of poverty, chastity and obedience, simple vows, as opposed to the solemn vows we would hope to take later on. But I felt I was a real seminarian now as the bus crossed into Dublin and turned up Whitehall Road, turning in at the great gate of Kimmage Manor. A great old mansion, and a vast seminary. In Templeogue, in Dublin west.

Because, novice to the time, I was part of it,
the harmony, the certitude, the uplift –
because I had traipsed in, from sea-cliffs and sea-roar
to the walled garden of the Song of Songs – I prayed

*kindle in me*
*the fires of your love.* I would
go up in flames and leave
a charred patch on the earth.

Kimmage Manor, seminary, was very different to Kilshane, novitiate. We were leaving behind the relative intimacy of the group of novices who had prayed and walked together for the best part of a year. We had left the warmth and security of a conservatory for the free-fall slopes of a seminary where the seminarians were hardened to such a life. We were now to merge with some three hundred others, seminarians studying philosophy, studying for various degrees in university, studying theology – as well as the teachers and masters of the seminary, and a goodly number of priests who had returned from the missions because of age, or ill health. These revered elders lived apart in what was called the 'White House', on the same grounds. The seminary building was huge, U-shaped, one side for 'philosophers', the other for the more advanced, the more saintly, the more worldly – 'theologians', each man with his own small room, his 'cell'. There were three floors to each building, and the chapel itself was great, laid out in choir shape, stalls facing each other across a central aisle, philosophers on one side, theologians on the other, two side aisles and a great choir loft with a massive organ, a high altar that looked to me like the forecourts of the Vatican itself. Oh yes we were cowed again, lost on a new shore, facing a greater ocean in which we had to learn to swim.

Perhaps for the first time, in this new season of my living, I began to grow aware of where I was, and of who I was. I had left the Ireland of forge and country dance hall, of braces, corsets, the mission, sin, the sea, the wide and free-range heathsides of the island, and was now wandering down clerestories in a sacred daze. It had become a question, at this point, of knowing a little better what I was doing, putting on the Christ as if he were soutane and stock and collar, old man, new man, overcoat. I still relished the sweet and sensual softness of dusk-light, the soothing

---

darkness of the trees along the driveway. I still sang my heart out in the lift and sway of the chant that clouded my mind with its beauty and high-rise rhythms.

We were summoned, the newly-born, into a room with the Director. Our names were called out, one by one, and we were told our position over the next few years. Those who were thought more able to study were held in Kimmage Manor for two years work on philosophy, through Latin, mind!, such subjects as Thomist epistemology, cosmology, theodicy, the history of philosophy through the writings of Frederick Copleston, logic ... *a priori* and *a posteriori, ens ut sic* ... and how to refute every possible type of error from atheism to communism and everything in between ...

Daunting indeed, and I was to be one of those to undertake such studies. It was autumn of 1962; I was nineteen years of age. (Marilyn Monroe had died in tragic circumstances and the more worldly older denizens of Kimmage Manor told us of this sad thing. I prayed my heart out for her.) The others were to spend three years – even four – cycling in and out to University College Dublin, then at Earlsfort Terrace in the heart of the city, there to undertake simple and advanced degrees in subjects that would enable them to teach, either in the Irish Holy Ghost colleges such as Rockwell, Blackrock and St Mary's, or in colleges abroad, on the missions, in Africa, or in Mauritius, or Trinidad. And our vows of obedience forbade any argument against the task we had each been allotted.

So began the two years of my life that were, perhaps, the strangest. I seem to have gone into a kind of happy slumber, moving pleasantly through the studies where all the books were in Latin (apart from Copleston and his comprehensive history of philosophy) and all our classes consisted in translating them and listening to the Fathers elucidate them. Almost all of which elucidation I promptly forgot. We developed, if that's the word, the prayers and silences of the novitiate, and spent our periods of recreation walking, in threes, round and round a cinder track that circled a small playing field. Sometimes we played basketball, having amongst us a great Trinidadian expert in that game. Sometimes we, philosophers, took on the theologians in rugby, where philosophy and theology were flung aside for the exuberance of sheer physical bravado and aggression. We spent time too in 'manual labours', gathering potatoes from the extensive fields about Kimmage Manor, thinning turnips, onions, carrots ...

And, of course, there was the music. It was the music that lifted me – those male voices raised into the sacred chant, like a wood of poplars blown this way by the breeze then that, following rites the way the poplars yield to necessary force; Gregorian chant, the long-drawn alleluias, the essential polyphonies of Palestrina, the flow of antiphon and responsorial; so many of us that we formed a fair field, surpliced and in choir, and I imagined our God sitting in his comfort chair, eyes closed and hands resting across his paunch, delighting in it, dispensing grace and glory to us privileged – though later I came to know that what I felt was my own elated being relishing the music and relishing it mostly beyond God's listening.

Out of some three hundred – perhaps a hundred more – young men in the seminary, there was no great difficulty in forming an excellent four-part harmony choir of real worth, and we were trained and directed by a priest well-known in Dublin in serious musical circles. So our singing of the Office, the hours, became almost professional, and the High Masses were so well done that they were occasionally broadcast on the national airwaves. Further, as I had studied music in Achill and in secondary school, and had achieved a high grade in my examinations in piano, I was added to a small number of organists and given special opportunities to develop my skills.

The organ was an exquisite one, recently electrified so there was no need to have someone there to pump the handle up and down, to give the organ breath. You flicked a switch and could hear, at once, the breathing, there, ready to respond to your lightest touch. There were three manuals, and pedals, and as I grew more expert at the task it became one of the greatest joys of that strange time to be alone in the great chapel, the might of that organ responsive to my hands and feet. I was nervous, of course, when the choir and choirmaster crowded up on to the gallery and I had to accompany the chanting, the singing, and play an occasional 'voluntary', either during the Communion or at the solemn exit from the church. But there was time set aside for the organists to have the gallery to ourselves, to practise, and those were the moments of great blessing, of personal and selfish gratification. As I grew more proficient and more confident, so the joys and the sometimes near ecstasy of the playing took me over. And occasionally, though rarely, the great space of the chapel below was empty, no worshipper present, and then the organist could give himself wholly to the music, to daring, to the great power of the organ.

I had been playing Bach on the great organ –
'A mighty fortress is our God' –
the church below me empty in the nowhere afternoon,
bombarde, clarion, celeste

and when I lifted fingers from the keys
it was, for a moment, eternity, and the walls of the world
contained nothing but the lingering breadth of the harmony,

rafters of the loft had lifted while the whole sky
trembled in a breeze that rippled slow across it
till all I knew was the touch of the fingers of Jesus

soft on my fingertips, my body
consciously drawing breath, my bones
refusing their earthy weight, and my soul
ringing with immortality.

Such rich moments were the music of that dream-period, that real and unreal world in which I lived and moved and had my being. Who was this Christ? this 'lover'? this crucified? to whom I was devoting all my days. Still I did not know. Nor did it seem to matter, for in the deepest ground of my being there was the God with whom I had been brought up, whom I accepted as naturally as I accepted breathing, whom I took for granted to be that Deity who had created the world, as the Bible outlined in the book of Genesis, that Deity who had dominated this world forever, who sat enthroned: Yahweh, God Almighty, Sovereign Lord and King; who had sent his Son to redeem us, a Son whose sacrifice on the cross God had willed, and accepted as a payment for all our sins; that Deity who had dominated through all the bright and the dark ages, whom we hymned in 'Faith of our Fathers', to which we would be true till death, in spite of dungeon, fire and sword. All of that accepted, never questioned, and still a dream to which I thought I had committed myself.

We took our meals in silence, listening to someone reading from the high lectern. Always the martyrology: a long list of names, in Latin, announced as saints and martyrs, offered to us, I presumed, as models whom we would be blessed to emulate. We shared the refectory, that large hall that held so many long tables, catering for our hundreds of young men, a high table at the head of the hall where the priests dined, watching down on us. Each moment, each activity, all to be devoted to the service of that distant God. Sometimes there was merriment during mealtime when the theologians, nearing their ordination, gave us 'sermons' as they rehearsed for their life as priests. And many of these were so badly constructed, so many errors made, so many words and phrases mispronounced, that we found great humour in them and they lifted our spirits into the routines of the day. Indeed, in the seminary, laughter was easy and easily found, as the life, I now know, was so utterly removed from the world outside that even our minds, our discussions, our dreams were birthed and berthed in the unreal where laughter kept us, at times, afloat.

I studied hard, theodicy, epistemology, all sorts of subjects. I took my place in the study hall where silence and the intense concentration of scholars were conducive to deep meditative reading. Or, I have to say, to dozing and a gentle, manly snoring. But I found interest in perusing the thousands of books that lined the walls of that large, long study hall, delving as deeply as I could into Mary, the Mother of God, my special Protectress, my Mother. I was all the more devoted to her as my birthday was the 8th of December, the great feast day of her Immaculate Conception which, of course, I scarcely understood. O Mary conceived without sin, pray for us who have recourse to thee. And each day died with sleep, as always, and before sleep the *'nunc dimittis'*, the canticle of Simeon who held the baby Jesus in his arms and knew that now he could rest forever in God's own arms.

> *Now I lay me down to sleep …*
> I folded my arms over my heart:
>
> prayed: Oh Lover crucified! and eased my soul
> to a blessed metaphysical darkness, entering
>
> original, essential loneliness. Exhausted
> after exercises of the soul I prayed
>
> *nunc dimittis servum tuum, Domine …*

Dreams evaporate, however slowly, like the dewfall in a weak sunlight. Since my baptism I had been assaulted with all the weaponry of the medieval Roman Catholic Church, its rules and regulations, its laws and strictures, its negativity about 'the world', its hierarchical dictatorship in so many forms. I was maturing with a sorry slowness, but I was maturing. At the end of my two years of philosophy I was almost as naïve and uneducated in the reality of living as I had always been; I had been cocooned and molly-coddled for two decades already. Now things began to change.

❧

Should a two-year course in philosophy not have made me capable of thinking for myself? Of course it should, but not the course that I had completed. What was given to me was taken out of a treasure chest of received and unquestioned tenets and teachings that I was to fill my back-packs with, from which I was to dispense more of the same, arguments, laws, regulations, awareness of sins, knowledge of graces ... all predetermined over the ages, to be shared out unchanged until the end of time. This was to presume that thinking and living and spirituality would not alter, nor change, nor develop, nor evolve. The first signal to me that this God who was supposed to be revered and served under such a weight of backpacks, was a distant, regal, imperial God, that personal living and development, 'edification' – or self-building – was already sorted ('saucered and blowed' as an old Dublin saying has it, referring to a cup of hot tea allowed to cool on a saucer by blowing on it), was the sailing by at an unconscionable distance of my Archbishop, the Prince Royal, John Charles McQuaid. He came to perform ordinations; there were military outriders, a police motorcycle escort, a Rolls Royce, and a great personage treated with the utmost pomp and ceremony. I know that on that day a tiny seed of personal anxiety dropped on the hard soil of my being, where it would undergo a moistening and softening before it could sprout into something wholly different. I was later to read, in Eckhart Tolle, of those 'inherited collective mind-patterns that have kept humans in bondage' for eons.

Faith in Christ, I have come to know, and true service of the person of Jesus the Christ, is not a question of rules and regulations, laws and immemorial tenets and arguments. I have come to see that the God I had believed in was a God of negatives – this 'apophatic' theology I was open to, or, as Scotus wrote, 'We do not know what God is, God Himself does not know what he is because he is not anything; God is not, because he transcends being': oh dear, oh dear; this unchanging God, this un- reachable God, this unfeeling God, this God that does not suffer ...

It has taken decades to feel that witness to the living grace and wonder that is Christ is a question of acceptance and confession, of self-surrender in a consciousness of personhood. Faith is impossible to underline with reason and argument; religions are where the rules and regulations apply. The word 'religion': does it mean a set of rules and regulations designed by a specific Church? and the word 'faith': does that suggest the personal response to God? But in my religion at that time, where was the radiance, where was the splendour, where was the possibility of personal love? I had been studying and swallowing whole a series of abstractions and propositions, of apologetics (in Latin, by the way), and had not yet begun to experience (through immaturity) any personal struggle. Yet my upbringing on Achill Island, in the splendour and radiance of that island, had given me a personal and very deep love of creation and the notion that behind such a creation was a Creator would be impossible to shift. When the world moved, when history lurched, and in the latter half of the twentieth century it lurched dramatically, then the rational abstractions and propositions, even if they were based on truth, could not withstand the movements, towards good or evil, that emerged. Where was my poor epistemology before the growing wealth and economies of Tiger Ireland? Where would my poor theodicy be before the onslaught of atheism that seemed to be the essence of freedom in the new age? Doctrines, apologetics, positions ... these are not what we live by; we live by love, we love by knowing radiance, radiance comes from the naïveté and the imaginative flights of the soul.

It took me a long time to figure out that the God I had been introduced to, the God I had studied, the God I hoped was on my side, was nothing more than the God of the ancient Greek Philosophers, that God who had no personal truck with the world, its people or its existence, a God that was, indeed, the ultimate source of all things, including myself, but who was so perfect in himself that he could have no truck with anything less than his own being. *Ens ut sic.* He was unchanging; he was eternal; he rested solely in himself. My philosophy told me this God was the unmoved mover of all things. He was the unchangeable source. He could not be stirred nor approached nor really understood. Yet for centuries this was the God who had been the great mountain range that believers had to try and climb. And Jesus, the person, the man, the human ... he stood for that God, that God made a sacrifice of him, subjecting him to an abject death and a most humiliating suffering so that the God of stone could deign to accept humanity back into some sort of relationship with him ... Oh dear, I was fed on abstractions; I swallowed them whole.

Myron Bradley Penner, in *The Christian Century* of July 2013, writes: 'Will someone who believes they have heard God speak bother to make clever arguments, brilliantly piecing together the evidence, so that the rational inescapability of the message is shown to be universally, objectively and neutrally justified?' A confession of personal conviction (a conviction always hovering, as it may, on the edge of doubt) is far more true to our living than a logical argument.

But that is now; it was not so, in my mind, then.

> At night, in my small cell, the world beyond
> bathed in silence under an eloquent moon, I lay
> sleepless, breathing a loneliness not spoken of
> in the texts, and though intelligent of the ordered
> mechanisms of your universe, in my own soul
> disorder swelled and I found
> nothing in mind or body that would answer
> questions I could not find the words to frame.

Moses spoke: 'Surely, this commandment that I am commanding you today is not too hard for you, nor is it too far away. It is not in heaven, that you should say, 'Who will go up to heaven for us, and get it for us so that we may hear it and observe it?' Neither is it beyond the sea, that you should say, 'Who will cross to the other side of the sea for us, and get it for us so that we may hear it and observe it?' No, the word is very near to you; it is in your mouth and in your heart for you to observe.' (Deut. 30:11–14)

*A Fledgling Saint*

In the long, hushed library of the seminary
I was copying out the signs and signals

left littered across our spirit-scapes by the busy
Fathers of the Church: Saint Anthony Abbot,

Saints Polycarp and Chrysostom and Aquinas,
pages from one of our eleven thousand tomes

touching from the serpent to the horses
of the Apocalypse. Always at my back I sensed

the old scribes with their pigments, the elaborate
whorls of their visions, but for me there was only

the next-to-silent scritching of a pen; under high
and narrow windows, radiators ticked, and I thought

of those saints, with the self-swallowing, fabulous
animals of their lettering, their blaeberry wimberry

texturings, who welcomed penances in their cells,
self-flagellation, their fingers hooked, the crozier-

crook of their spines over their cold
library of seven books. Soon I would walk –

the *liber usualis* in my hand – on narrow corridors,
keeping always, in humility, close against the walls,

eyes in custody, to sing out vespers, compline,
relishing the long, hushed centuries of the plainsong,

anticipating the comforts of a silent, and a long, night:
*in manus tuas Domine commendo spiritum meum.*

## Seminarian, with Raleigh Bike

⬥

Late in the summer of 1963 I was called to the office of the Father Dean of Studies and told that I was being sent to University College, Dublin, where I would study physics and chemistry and get a BSc so that I would be able to teach in a Holy Ghost school, should the need arise. Another seminarian, Jerome McCarthy, was told to go to University College, Dublin, to study French and English, with the same end in mind. My heart sank. Jerome's heart sank. Jerome had done very well in science in secondary school; I had been useless at it. Jerome felt he was hopeless at languages and was not well versed in literature. I knew I was fairly good at languages; I loved literature. But – we had vowed obedience. We met, somewhat surreptitiously, to talk to one another about it. We agreed, without hesitation, that we had to swap studies. But who would go to the superior? Who would bell the cat? We went together. I had been led to believe that even if we were asked by our superiors to go out and plant cabbages upside down, that we should go and do it; the will of the superior was the will of God. We put our case. Father gazed at us for a while. Then he dismissed us. It was a come back tomorrow situation, and we left. I went straight to the chapel; I prayed, perhaps more fervently than ever, to a God I hoped might have some heart, to that God we had prayed to in Achill for fine weather, to the God we prayed to when we needed the county of Mayo to do well in the Connacht final.

He heard my prayer.

So I began a three-year course of study in University College, Dublin, then at Earlsfort Terrace near the heart of the city. I took English and French, cycling in each morning, rain, sun, snow, frost (obedience, of course), wearing my black suit, white shirt, blue stock and priestly collar. I had to wear that black priestly hat, too, and sometimes a black, priestly coat. A companion from the novitiate, Maurice Piat, cycled with me, in and out, and we spent most of the day together as he, too, was studying French and English. He had come to Kilshane from Mauritius where, I gathered, his family were quite well off, but he had little English when he arrived; I became a sort of tutor to him in English and, of course, he helped me with my French.

Suddenly, the world was opening up before me, and it was wonderful. I forget the names of my French lecturers, but in English I was lucky to study with Seamus Deane, Denis Donoghue, Maurice Harmon, John Jordan, Augustine Martin … and the very rich island of English literature began to offer me its treasures. I read voraciously. Back in the library in Kimmage Manor, I continued to pursue those studies, the questions of faith, the presence of Christ, now somewhat sidelined, of necessity. Still, life as a philosopher-seminarian continued, praying the hours, working on my skills as an organist, carrying out my functions in the running of the seminary. I was wholly occupied and the days and weeks and months began to slide by, my focus outwards as well as inwards.

For a season I worked in the bicycle shed. There were at least seventy bicycles in the shed, for the use of the many seminarians studying in Earlsfort Terrace, and they needed to be kept in reasonable running order. They were numbered, a bicycle assigned, with its lock and key. My function was repairing punctures, fixing broken spokes, chains, brakes; I tried to straighten buckled wheels and, in the rare moments when all the bicycles were running smoothly, I and another seminarian, worked to 'build' another bicycle out of the dismembered parts of the failed machines. It was fun; it was absorbing; it was oily. And afterwards I had to rush my prayers, rush my ablutions, change into my university suit and cycle off to my lectures.

Anglo-Saxon literature intrigued me; we translated it into modern English, but it left a direct and simple message on my soul, that the sound-patterns of language, the spokes and chains and oils of language, are vital to the working of a poem. The robust and muscular, sometimes rough, sounds of Anglo-Saxon appealed to my Achill Island ear; the essentially Christian emphasis in the literature of that period rang heartily in my own soul. It was there that poetry, at last, entered my spirit in a meaningful way though it would yet take years for me to move further in my love of that art. Courses in English fiction left me somewhat confused, so much of it to be taken on board, so little time in the course of one person's life, to absorb it all. More modern English poetry touched me, in those years, less closely. I associated poetry with a genius that was simply gifted from on high and never to be emulated; Wordsworth, Tennyson, Hardy, Eliot … these were as remote and wonderful to me as the prophets who stalked the world of the Old Testament, who heard the word of God calling to them, demanding the dedication of their lives and a listening faculty that could never, ever be mine. American poetry, as offered by Denis Donoghue and others, left me cold; it was presented as intellectual, or extreme, and did not seem to emerge from any sort of meaningful world. But there was, in those years, a new and strong movement towards what was called 'Anglo-Irish' literature and there the sound of poetry that I knew to be bronze and militant, came to me as tin-whistle, uilleann pipes music, nationalist and homely. In evening lecture series offered by such as Austin Clarke and John Montague, poetry began to appear as something possible, real, still prophetic but at the threshold of an ordinary life.

As yet my life was anything but ordinary, and religious topics were always to the fore in my home-place, at that time, of the seminary. We were encouraged still to study the lives of the saints, the great volumes of the Christian thinkers, the life of Jesus, the spirit of Mary. But, as we walked the grounds at break-times, our discussions moved more towards the works of T.S. Eliot, his mystical references clear to our seminarian minds, the poems of Crashaw and Herbert and Donne, their 'meta-physical' concerns chiming somewhat with our own seminary reading.

And then, one strange day, a shift came in my whole spirit. As usual, Maurice Piat and I cycled together down into the city. It was raining; we shook ourselves as dry as possible in the basement where we locked our bicycles and hung our wet priestly hats and coats into our assigned lockers. We took our French and English texts with us and climbed to the room where our next lecture in French was to take place. I was now in second year, having done quite well in my first exams. I was a real student, but still very much outside what would be known to most people as any university life.

We were on time. Maurice and I sat side by side. There were a few nuns there, too; we could nod to them but scarcely knew them. I glanced at Anna, a beautiful young woman – not a nun – who shared the French course but to whom I had never spoken, nor did she ever glance towards me. I have never been too good at 'custody of the eyes'; *if your right eye should cause you to stumble, gouge it out* … I had always willed to relish the beautiful things of the earth and when a beautiful woman passed close by, I was slow to heed the evangelists' calls. Our lecturer was late. Maurice took out a book that had come his way and showed it to me; it was short, in French; it was called *La messe sur le monde* and was written by somebody called Pierre Teilhard de Chardin. We placed the book between us and began to read. I was greatly taken by it and we finished it during the time the French lecture should have taken place; our lecturer, thankfully, did not show at all.

'Since, oh Lord, once more,' [it began] 'and no longer in the forests of the Aisne, but in the steppes of Asia, I have neither bread, nor wine nor altar, I will raise myself above the symbols to the pure majesty of the Real and will offer you, I your priest, on the altar of the whole Earth, the labour and the suffering of the world.'

I was brought up to believe in the seven-day wonder, that Genesis was factual, that all of creation was achieved as a one-off event, over seven days, some few thousand years ago ... Creationism. It was all done and achieved and all we've got to do is hold on to the rules and regulations devised by God himself (and the laws of the Church, and ...) to get us through the valley of suffering and out into Paradise at the far end. Teilhard de Chardin, that day, entered my soul and I began to believe that creation is an ongoing process, an evolution. Gradually, over the next few weeks, reading this little book over and over, there came into my consciousness a belief that the original seeds and resourcefulness of this created world are the power behind this evolution. And not only I, and every other human being, must move on, move forward, but the whole of creation takes its share in this evolution. Our earth, offered up to God with its joys and sorrows, movement of chance, surprise, collapse, decay – all of it creates a drama in which we live and move and have our being, and the final act is by no means written.

My chalice and my paten are the depths of a soul wide open to all the forces which, in a moment now, will rise from every point of the Globe and converge towards the Spirit – Let them come to me, the memory and the mystical presence of those whom the light awakens into a new day!

All of this was a revelation to me: but, of course, it was also a slow, slow dawning. The words entered my spirit where they settled, developed and eventually produced their fruits. With *La messe sur le monde* I began to search for other works of de Chardin's but could find very little, yet the references and quotations from his work by other writers, helped me put together a great deal more. (I found out, of course, that his superiors in the Jesuits, worried by his strange ideas, had forbidden him to write, and to teach.) In a nutshell (and remembering the image used by the mystic Julian of Norwich) I grew to know that our world is on its way to a better future. What became clear to me in that airless lecture room is that over the last centuries in particular, the movement has been one towards developing complexity, a deeper and wider consciousness, a drawing closer of all humanity, and the possibilities of more meaningful and lasting freedom.

> I wish that at this moment my being might resonate to the deep murmur of the agitated world, this human Ocean whose immensity terrifies us and brings trouble into the hearts of even the most fervent believers. All that will increase in the World, during this day, all that will diminish – and all that will die – this, Lord, is what I gather up into myself to offer them to you; this is the matter of my sacrifice, the only one that you desire.

And I felt, glowing within me, a sense that all the physical universe I had loved and cherished in my younger years, might form a sacred part of human living, and might not be cast into exterior darkness as a snare for the soul of humankind. *La messe sur le monde* had given me the grace to understand the workings of Creation far beyond the hesitations and misunderstandings I had known when first faced with the 'threat' of Darwin's discoveries. I was given – as yet merely trembling with potency in my spirit – a firm ideological basis for understanding the ongoing evolution of mankind. I was able to see the entire universe as one great process of becoming. Teilhard called it 'cosmogenesis'. A new faith began to dawn in me, a faith that this beautiful world, this Ireland, this earth in all its wonder and in all its grieving, must be the place in which our human lives take root and grow and without a deep rooting in this earth, how could the spirit ever come to maturity and to a real awareness of the majesty and power and love of the Creator. And what would be my position and my role in this ongoing evolution? A priest, a missionary to Africa or Latin America in the Congregation of the Holy Ghost? I was no longer so sure.

## Seminarian, with Chisel and Saw

෨෧

My life as unquestioning seminarian was getting a little fraught by the middle of my second year in university. The word one would have used was 'lax': I was growing lax. By now my parents had moved from Achill to Dublin, my grandmother, Nanna, was ill and was soon moved into the hospice in Harolds Cross, at that time insensitively known as 'the hospice for the dying'. My route by bicycle from Kimmage to Earlsfort Terrace, passed the gate of the hospice and I was permitted to visit. It was a very sad and difficult time; Nanna was suffering; she was very elderly and at times, when I called in, she did not really know who I was. At other moments she did know me, and expressed great pride in showing off her grandson, going to be a priest. I already had doubts about this but, of course, I did not express these doubts to her. Nor was I certain what exact shape these doubts were taking.

I had also moved from functioning in the bicycle shed, to carpentry. Another seminarian and I were given the run of a workshop which had all the carpentry tools one's heart might desire. Our task was to build some free-standing library shelves, a two-sided affair, sloping in towards the top, shelves on either side, about five feet high and built on wheels. It was a delightful challenge and Charlie and I took to it with a will. 'Function' time was in the morning, after morning Mass, office, meditation, breakfast. Usually an hour was allocated to these tasks and Charlie and I put on our dungarees, took hold of our tools, and faced into our creative carpentry. We made ourselves familiar with bradawl and saw, chisel and plane, hand drill and mallet … all of which I had seen and tinkered with in grandfather Ted's workshop years ago. In our workshop we were, of course, allowed to speak and we consulted each other in great seriousness as to tongue-and-groove, dovetailing, bevel, chamfer, and down to the distant future where we would hope to varnish, stain or even French polish, our free-standing bookshelves on their castors.

I am aware, very much in hindsight, that I was moving in a state of some confusion. I was immersed in English and French literature; I was immersed in Thomas Aquinas, Augustine, the history of philosophy and the beginnings of theology. Out at university I moved among happy and confident young men and women who seemed to gaze, occasionally, askance at the hatted and collared and black-suited clerics who did not participate in any of the university societies or sports, who appeared in small groups, like a coven of crows, who moved along the corridors and in the lecture halls with their eyes cast down, who disappeared together as soon as lectures were over. But custody of the eyes was becoming ever more difficult and occasional discussions between clerics and lay students were inevitable and, I found, stimulating. Back in the Kimmage library I found my studies moving from Voltaire and Rousseau to T.S. Eliot and George Herbert, from eschatology as outlined in the gospel of Matthew to Mariology and Christology. In October of 1962, when I first came to Kimmage Manor, the Second Vatican Council was opened and we heard rumbles about 'windows being thrown open', about modernising the Church, there was murmuring of the backsliding and ignorance of traditionalism. I was young. I was still hopelessly immature. I was confused. I was helplessly confused. I was living in the bleak desert between two ages.

My brother Declan was, at this time, in the Jesuit seminary in Milltown Park, just across the city, but we rarely met. Many decades after this time Declan told me that one day he was called to the parlour of Milltown Park, that his brother wanted to see him. I had cycled from Kimmage Manor to Milltown, he told me, having got permission to come and speak with my brother on some difficulties I was having. I have absolutely no memory of that afternoon. It appears we sat together, awkwardly, on stiff chairs, Declan a Jesuit, I a Holy Ghost, both of us in clerical garb, and we talked and Declan never got the remotest idea of why I had come over. It appears I kept looking at my watch and saying I would soon have to be back as I only had permission to visit up to five o'clock. He did tell me we spoke about our Nanna in the hospice, and how hurt and worried we were. Still I have no memory of the visit. I expressed no anxieties, doubts or confusion to him, and I left him as unenlightened as I was myself, as to why I had come. Oh dear. I was confused.

I called in to see Nanna one day, sometime later, this I do remember, on my way back to the seminary. It was an afternoon of bright sunlight. A Sister who met me at the front door became all fussy, insisting on calling me 'Father', and being distinctly obliging and assiduous in her language and obsequious in her movements. Proudly she showed me into the ward. Nanna was sitting out on a chair beside her bed; there were flowers in a bowl on the window-sill and the sunlight lay like a bright curtain across the highly-polished floor. She seemed to be in good form and she asked me all about Kimmage Manor, my studies, what stage was

I at, and I know she was wondering, wondering when and if I should ever reach ordination. I found it difficult to tell her, but I did, as she seemed alert and strong enough to understand; that Declan had moved on, in his Jesuit studies, and was now in France, in Chantilly, and would be there for some three years. Suddenly she stopped, gazed over at the window for a moment, and sighed deeply. I glanced up, too; in the distance we could just about make out the tops of trees, the soft clouds scarcely moving, a few birds, gulls or jackdaws moving by.

'When are you taking me out of here?' she asked me, abruptly, taking my hand in hers. I looked into her face and there were tears moving slowly down over her gentle, ever-kindly face. I was distressed. What could I say? 'I miss you all,' she went on. 'I miss the house, the chores, I would love to be in the kitchen, my apron on, cooking, I miss that, I miss my own room, I miss the garden, I miss the lake behind the house, I miss the postman coming up the road, I miss Declan and Ted, and I know the workshop out the back must be in a bad state, a bad state.' She was chafing my fingers between her hands, the tears were moving freely down and I sensed that she believed she was in Achill still, and that it was in our hands, even mine, to take her back into her loved and accustomed way of living. 'You will be a priest, soon, soon,' she said. And then, glancing about carefully to see who was listening, she went on: 'You might talk to the head nun here, she's nice, and kind, she'll let me go home, if you ask her, if you ask her for me. You will ask her, won't you, Jackie, you will ask her?'

'Yes,' I replied, fully determined to speak to the Sister. 'Yes, I promise I will ask her.' And Nanna smiled at me, and for a moment I could see her again as I had known and loved her, that intensely lived-in face alert with kindness towards others, and yet burdened with her own ongoing cares.

By the time I left her that afternoon, she seemed to have moved back a little into a quiet absence; she was humming to herself, and had forgotten that I was there. I stood for a while outside the ward, there in the corridor. Outside the hospice window there was a garden, neat and ordered, box hedges beautifully shaped, pebbled walkways between. On the window ledge, there before me, was a plaster statue of Mary Immaculate, her eyes raised towards the ceiling, a set of rosary beads about her fingers. And at her feet a small vase of blue flowers, of green grasses. I was hurt, for Nanna, for myself; I was hurt, by the world, by its inevitable pain and its sorrow. I went out into the foyer, but there was nobody there, except for an old man who seemed to be taking care of the desk. He was reading a newspaper. I thought of asking him if I could speak with the head nun, but it seemed pointless and somewhere inside me I knew how futile and saddening it would be. I postponed my visit to her, promising myself, and reiterating my promise, in my mind, to Nanna, that I would speak to her next time, before going in to the ward.

There was no next time. Within three or four days my Father Superior called me into his office and told me she had died. He was gentle with me, but very matter-of-fact. He sympathised; he asked me had I known her well; he told me the arrangements, the Mass in the hospice, the funeral taking her from there to the cemetery in Malahide, out in the far suburbs of Dublin. I felt like crying in front of him: Malahide! But, I was going to say, but! her husband Ted is lying in Bunnacurry graveyard, among fuchsia flowers and oxeye daisies, where the bees haunt and where robins flick their bodies peacefully about; you can hear the Atlantic from that graveyard, I wanted to say, and sometimes the bog cotton shifts like a swarm of white butterflies; there is quiet, and peace, old clay pipes and sea-shells, dark green bottles with long-stemmed lilies speaking glad memories to the dead. And there is space for her, a lot of space kept there for her. But I said none of that. Nor do I ever remember asking my parents, why Malahide? Why Malahide?

Father Superior was kind enough to say the Mass, and to accompany the cortege on its long, sad journey across the city northwards to the suburb of Malahide. 'You will say the prayers over the grave,' he told me. 'Bring your soutane, your surplice, your biretta, your lectionary. Say the prayers, in a firm voice, you will be her minister there, you will show her how you loved her, by your prayers, your strength, your certainties that she is in a better place, with her God. You will scatter the holy water into the grave, you will drop the first handful of clay, you will lead us in the decade of the rosary. The resurrection. I will be near you. You will do well.'

And I did well. But I was hurting. I was confused. I stood tall. She would have been proud of me. In spite of the breeze in from the estuary I spoke the prayers aloud and firmly. I scattered the drops of water onto her grave from a small plastic bottle. I dropped a tiny sprinkle of clay onto the coffin, hating that scrabbling sound down on the polished wood below. I said a decade of the rosary and counted the ten Hail Marys calmly and with dignity. And all the time what I wanted to do was to cry, loudly and freely, and to be held and consoled by someone I loved, and who loved me. And as I turned away from her plot I think it was the moment I knew that I was in the wrong place, in the wrong position, that my faith and hope and charity were not built on a sure enough foundation to see me through the rest of my life as a priest, alone, and in the service of others. I felt guilty, guilty for living, guilty for not loving her enough, guilty of sin, guilty of dust.

I was confused. Seminary life continued for me. I made no decisions. I carried on. I went to university. I carried out all my duties. But I was shaken through. And one morning, as Charlie and I continued work on our library free-standing shelves, I was labouring over a piece of wood and getting it into size and shape for our task. There were tears, just a little weeping, but it was enough to blur my eyesight for a moment. I was using a chisel. Like a fool I made the most obvious mistake one can make with a chisel, holding the tool in my right hand, holding the piece of timber in my left, just in front of the chisel. The chisel slipped and cut deeply into the index finger of my left hand. It did not hurt, just a slight stinging pain. For a long moment, Charlie and I simply stood aghast, watching the blood come rushing out of my finger. I dropped the chisel, grabbed a handkerchief and wrapped it tightly about my finger. Charlie came with me to the nurse. She cleaned the wound, put some stuff on it, did not stitch it; then she bandaged it and told me it would be ok. She told me, too, how foolish I was, and I agreed with her. Foolish indeed. Charlie had to finish the shelves by himself. I still have a gently curved healing mark on my finger, quite visible, quite a fine memorial to foolishness, good will and confusion.

Further confusion followed. During the summer months, the seminarians were allowed to go to the beach, in a group. The chosen spot was Portmarnock, on the other side of the city, not far from Malahide. We were to go by bicycle, of course, perhaps twenty of us on a chosen day. On the bikes we were to carry a tent in which we might change into modest bathing costumes, up in the sand-dunes behind the beach. We carried all sorts of equipment suitable for a day out, for our camping: a first aid kit!, can openers, matches, camping stove, a hamper with sandwiches, with sausages, with gas refills, pots and pans ... the works, all bundled and packaged carefully on our bicycles, but making the long cycle of several miles very difficult and, of course, a little hazardous. After at least an hour's cycling, we were to set up on the back of the beach, preferably half-hidden in the dunes, swim, eat, play our manly games, pack up, and cycle back. Arrive for Vespers and Compline in no fit state ... sweating, sand in our shoes, salt on our skins, weariness in our bones.

I thought of the Vatican Council's wish to 'fling the windows open to the world'. My family were now resident in Dublin. I phoned my father in the morning and he drove to Kimmage, parked the car outside the bicycle shed. Through the open window I passed the heaviest of our camping equipment, a tent, the stove, the hamper, such items, then Father drove three of us out to Portmarnock, we set up the stuff while the others cycled more easily out along the coast road; Father left, and came back in the evening to take the heavy matter back to the seminary. It was common sense. It was rational. It made the day pleasant and restful. It was unheard of. It was against all the rules. It was never to happen again. I was severely scolded. I did not feel that I had in any way sinned, it was nowhere in the rules and constitution that common sense was not to be followed ... Or perhaps it was: there were always those cabbage plants to be planted upside down in the sand.

Early in the beginning of the new scholastic year, I made up my mind; I would leave. The decision was not difficult, but the actual process of leaving was not made simple. I had to get dispensation from the Order, from Rome (I was told, but was not sure), I had to be dispensed of my vows of poverty, chastity and obedience. I spent hours with my spiritual director, a fine and human priest who had returned from the missions and knew what life was about. But he urged me to stay; was I sure now that I had no vocation? How could I be sure? What about putting your hand to the plough and turning back? Would God be disappointed in me? Would my family be disappointed? Would I be disappointed in myself? He suggested, at length, as I held firmly to my decision, that I might leave for a year, take a job 'in the world', then come back and take up where I had left off. That seemed worse than ever to me; one foot in the world, the other in the seminary; that would not work for me. Then he sent me to see a psychiatrist – a priest lecturer in University College, Dublin. I went in to this priest's room in trepidation but was welcomed with great warmth. General chit-chat about the weather, about my English and French studies, about the all-Ireland football finals.

'Now,' he said at last, folding his hands in his lap and sitting up straight, facing me where I sat uncomfortably, ill-at-ease in spite of his gentleness; 'I have one question for you and I want you to answer quickly, without hesitation. Right?'

I nodded.

'Do you want to stay in the Holy Ghost Fathers?'

'No, Father,' burst out of me, an impetuous answer, so obviously from my heart and soul that he smiled at me and began to write a note to my superiors. Within the week, I was to be back in the world, a layman, a failure? A misfit?

I was sent, all secretly of course, lest I disturb the other seminarians, into the centre of the city, to Clerys store where the Holy Ghost Fathers had an account. I was measured for a suit; I took one off the pegs. It was an ugly brown, with a slender stripe of grey through it. It would do. I bought a shirt, a tie, brown shoes. I wrapped it all up in a brown paper parcel and somehow smuggled it back into Kimmage Manor. Next day, when all the others were in the library, or in the chapel singing Lauds, I dressed in my new gear; I packed some stuff into my old suitcase; I placed my heavy crucifix that had been given to me as a postulant, a lifetime back, on top of my shirts, vests, underwear. I gazed around my cell, sighed deeply, said a prayer to Nanna to help me, and closed the door on my vocation.

Half an hour later I was standing, confused still, at the bus stop on Whitehall Road, waiting for the 15A to take me into town. There I took the 9 to Drumcondra and walked down Griffith Avenue to my father and mother, a 'spoiled priest'.

> Mid-morning, when the others were at Lauds,
> I crept away, a small suitcase in my hand,
> down the marble stairway and out beneath yew trees
> to wait, under the high wall, for a bus
> into the city. I see it, not as failure, but as your way
> of weaning me from poesies of the island
> to the dry mathematics of your concerns. I was welcomed
> home. Strange place. Strange comforts. A stranger
> on the bleak island of the world and in its rhythms

you faded to a dim, a medieval legend. Still
I walk these shores a stranger, my gaze
wandering out over the ocean, caught again
by the mysteries of kittiwake, puffin, auk.


I was welcomed home with love and care; there was no reproach, not
a hint of it. If my last year or two had been struggling between two ages,
now I was clear of that and was beginning, at last, to reach my own,
proper age. I continued in my final year at University College, Dublin,
still close to Maurice Piat, who did not reproach me either. But Nanna, I
wondered, how she would have thought of it, would she have been hurt,
disappointed? Or would she have known how confused and hurt I had
become? I believed, and still believe, she would have known my pains;
and perhaps, was it her plot I stood over out at Malahide that sorry day?
Her 'plot'? And at Christmas I rejoiced in a fine set of Old Spice
aftershave, deodorant, and body wash.


*The Pride of Life*
   *for Tim Sheehan*

McGarvey and I were young and male and speaking
of the concupiscence of eyes, of flesh,
of the pride of life; our God, old Taskmaster,
demanded of us perfection, suffering and Latin.

McGarvey and I were dressing boards
of flesh-coloured deal, dovetailing them
into library shelves when the chisel,
curved like the quarter moon, slipped, and sliced

into my index finger; maladroit, I watched
blood spurt until the pain scalded me
and I sat down, stunned, amongst wood-shavings
and white dust; *in illo tempore* seminarians,

McGarvey and I (like Christ himself) were in otherwhere
on carpentry assignment, though I was more
for the study of Aquinas and the Four Last Things, more
apt with pen and paper and the ancient texts;

my finger-flesh had lifted and I tied it, tight,
with my seminarian's white handkerchief – *you're*
*pale as a ghost*, McGarvey said, that ghost
still with me now, pen in hand, wandering the world,

a fine-curved scar on my index finger;
a solitary gladiolus, elegant and tall,
of a cardinal brightness, beckons to me
from outside the window, and that young seminarian –

misfit and eager, trenchant and melancholy
in the pursuit of love – haunts me still, his God
and McGarvey's God, displaced, replaced, my God
untonsured now, and feminine, and here.

## Ordinary Possibilities

Thomas Merton wrote, speaking of poets: 'We remain innocent and
invisible to publicists and bureaucrats ...' He stated, too, that the artist
has inherited the combined functions, in our time, 'of hermit, pilgrim,
prophet, priest, showman, sorcerer, soothsayer, alchemist, and bonze'.
The artist needs to reject society's demands, but must guard against being
defined by this rejection. And Archbishop Rowan Williams adds, 'the
artist, like the monk, has an interior wilderness to discover'. Priest, monk;
hadn't I moved in that direction? Hadn't I found this was not quite for
me? And wasn't there a world I still had to find my way in? In this
context, too, Merton saw the human being the way Gregory of Nazianzus
spoke of him: 'earthly yet heavenly ... midway between majesty and
lowliness'. And each human being is *homo liturgicus*, a priest of nature,
the means of articulated theophany in the world, called to offer the world
back to the Creator in thanksgiving. Our freedom insists that each human
being has his or her own personal and peculiar destiny in which to
exercise a distinctive and unrepeatable way. Difficult to find, perhaps,
and many twists and turns, not to mention dead ends, along the way.
Merton wrote: 'My own individual destiny is a meeting, an encounter

with God that He has destined for me alone. His glory in me will be to receive from me something which he can never receive from anyone else.' All of this I seemed to know instinctively, though it took many years of writing, of trial and error, before such a 'vocation' became clear to me.

I taught secondary school for some ten years, English, French and Spanish. Through my university studies in English literature, and through my encounters with the work of Gerard Manley Hopkins, I fell in love with poetry, and with the notion of poetry. As I sought a meaningful way through life, I tried many things. I became organist and choirmaster in the large parish church of Whitehall in Dublin and enjoyed it. The choir was a four-part adult mixed-voice choir, about forty-five good souls, and we became good and fairly well known. We were chosen to sing a Mass on Eurovision, and the music was to be supplied by the Chieftains, already internationally known at this time. I wrote words for some of the parts of the Mass and Paddy Moloney wrote the music. We put it all together in a Mass which went over well on television; then we performed it a few times, in University College, Dublin, now out in Belfield, in University Church on Stephen's Green, at Listowel Writers' Week. Was this to be the direction I was to go in? I knew it was not, as my knowledge of music and my skills in playing organ or piano were not up to the standard I knew would be required. One piece remains from that Mass, and became the first poem I wrote that was published anywhere. It comes, of course, from *La messe sur le monde*, and the lovely notions of offering up to God the positives and the negatives of our human endeavours.

### Offertory

We offer you, Lord, in our strong, our sensitive hands
to-day this bread:
this plough and plod, soft coaxing, collecting,
    the mixing and moulding, dull rumbling of trucks
        till the creates all are named for those countless lands;
from our proud, proud hands, o Christ, accept this bread.

We offer you, Lord, in our soil-cracked, ours woollen hands
to-day this wine:
this fall, this crush, the strain, the pain

o crumbling collapsing of flesh and the fierce
    dizzy dash of the blood of those countless lands;
from our weary, weary hearts, o Christ, accept this wine.

Then give into our hands
   your flesh
      to melt and merge with the soil and stones,

and give into our hearts
   your blood
      to seep through the sweat when the world groans;

that our earth may grow through its brightest blackest parts
a sight well pleasing to the Lord of lands.

I was paid five shillings for the poem, and I was thrilled. I kept writing. I founded a musical society, also in Whitehall and we put on *The Pirates of Penzance* in the local hall. I was director, and conducted a small orchestra. It also went across very well. I began a small drama group in the parish, Anthos Players, and helped with the staging of two or three plays. Again I knew, in my heart, I was not going to develop in any of these areas, my hopeless self-consciousness militating against me in roles I felt were not truly natural to me. I was, deep down, a solitary; I could have been hermit (for a while!); I could have been anchorite (for a shorter while!). I kept writing. I read contemporary poetry and found I could hardly get any grip on it, being exercised for so long by the great tradition of formal English verse. But I persisted. And I kept writing. Very slowly I began to understand what was happening in poetry around me. I had a few more poems published. And yes, I kept writing. Achill Island remained firmly to the fore when I delved into my own being, trying to figure who and what I was.

*Basking Shark: Achill Island*

Where bogland hillocks hid a lake
we placed a tom-cat on a raft; our guns
clawed pellets in his flesh until, his back
arched, the pink tongue bitten through, he drowned.

We fished for gulls with hooks we'd hide
in bread and when they swallowed whole we'd pull;
screaming they sheared like kites above a wild
sea; twine broke and we forgot. Until
that day we swam where a great shark
glided past, dark and silent power
half-hidden through swollen water; stunned
we didn't shy one stone. Where seas lie calm
dive deep below the surface; silence there
pounds like panic and moist fingers touch.

As Thomas Merton wrote in *Raids on the Unspeakable*, 'Poetry is the flowering of ordinary possibilities. It is the fruit of ordinary and natural choice … We are the children of the Unknown. We are the ministers of silence that is needed to cure all victims of absurdity who lie dying of a contrived joy. Let us then recognise ourselves for who we are: dervishes mad with secret therapeutic love which cannot be bought or sold, and which the politician fears more than violent revolution, for violence changes nothing. But love changes everything.'

T. S. Eliot wrote: 'Real poetry survives not only a change of popular opinion but the complete extinction of interest in the issues with which the poet was passionately concerned.' If a nation ceases to produce great writers, especially great poets, the language and culture will deteriorate. By affecting the language one affects the sensibility of a nation. The possibility of regaining a religious poetic received impetus with the work of writers like Eliot, like R. S. Thomas, like Czeslaw Milosz, who wrote, in *A Year of the Hunter*: 'The mainstay of the Catholic Church appears to be the faithful who refrain from questioning, either because it's of no interest to them or because they have surrounded themselves beforehand with an impregnable barrier.' Serious questioners, he believed, inevitably become heretics. 'Poetry's separation from religion has always strengthened my conviction that the erosion of the cosmic-religious imagination is not an illusion and that the vast expanses of the planet that are falling away from Christianity are the external correlative of this erosion.'

Because of my background in faith on Achill Island, in Mungret College and in the Holy Ghost novitiate and seminary, religion for me was still not to be questioned. Perhaps, I thought, if I could write a poetry out of religious conviction, then I might be getting somewhere. It took me a long time to realise that poetry that begins with the notion of getting across an idea is not poetry, it is polemic. But I kept writing.

*Four*

*Winter in Meath*

❦

The first months of the year 1981 were blanketed, in Ireland, in snow and frost; the roads were almost impassable, the fields and gardens swallowed up in a shroud of white and, though the skies were clear and bright, the countryside of Meath, where I was then living, was a wonderland of white, difficult, beautiful, and I was hurting from the death of my young wife, Barbara.

*Winter in Meath*

Again we have been surprised
deprived, as if suddenly,
of the earth's familiarity

it is like the snatching away of love
making you aware at last you loved

sorrows force their way in, and pain
like memories half contained

the small birds, testing boldness, leave
delicate tracks
                    closer
to the back door

while the cherry flaunts blossoms of frost
and stands in desperate isolation

the base of the hedgerow is a cliff of snow
the field is a still of a choppy sea
white waves capped in a green spray

147

*John F. Deane*

a grave was dug into that hard soil
and overnight the mound of earth
grew stiff and white as stones flung onto a beach

our midday ceremony was hurried, forced
hyacinths and holly wreaths dream birds
appearing on our horizonless ocean

the body sank slowly
the sea closed over
things on the seabed stirred
again in expectation

this is a terrible desolation

the word 'forever'
stilling all the air

to glass

night tosses and seethes;
mind and body chafed all day
as a mussel-boat restlessly irritates
the mooring

on estuary water a fisherman
drags a long rake against the tide; one
snap of a rope and boat and this
solitary man
sweep off together into night

perhaps the light from my window
will register a moment with some god
riding by on infrangible glory

at dawn
names of the dead
appear on the pane

beautiful

in undecipherable frost

breath
hurts them
and they fade


the sea has gone grey as the sky
and as violent

pier and jetty go under
again and again
as a people suffering losses

a flock of teal from the world's edge
moves low over the water
finding grip for their wings along the wind

already among stones
a man
                       like a priest
stooping in black clothes
has begun beachcombing

the dead, gone silent in their graves
have learned the truth about resurrection


            you can almost look into the sun
            silver in the silver-blue monstrance
            cold over the barren white cloth of the world

            for nothing happens


149

> each day is an endless waiting
> for the freezing endlessness of the dark
>
> once – as if you had come across
> a photograph, or a scarf maybe – a silver
> monoplane like a knife-blade cut
> across the still and haughty sky
>
> but the sky healed up again after the passing that left
> only a faint, pink thread, like a scar

In 1973 I married Barbara Sheridan, daughter of the great comedian and Music-Hall artiste, Cecil Sheridan. We went on honeymoon, taking the car, and in North Wales visited St Beuno's, the Jesuit seminary where Gerard Manley Hopkins had studied for the priesthood and where he had written his most joyous and exciting poems. In April of 1975, our first child, Laura, was born but Barbara did not seem to be recovering. She became very ill and it wasn't until the 1st of May that the doctors told me they had discovered what the problem was, lupus, systemic lupus erythematosus, an autoimmune disease that can affect any and every part of the body. She was treated with steroids and the improvement was fast for a while, but there were side effects. Serious side effects. We entered a period of complicated and difficult illnesses, cures, recurrences. By the autumn of 1979 I had to give up teaching to be with her, with Laura and with our second daughter, Catherine, born in August of that year. We moved house, from Dublin, which we could no longer afford, to a small house in Mornington, County Meath, near the banks of the river Boyne. Barbara died on 23 December 1980, at the age of thirty-seven, from complications caused by lupus.

The chill of that long winter remains fixed in my memory and my imagination. I struggled with the emptiness. I tried to lift myself and our two daughters into some form of hope and joy. They were young, very young. The doctors had told me that lupus was not an inheritable disease. I believed the doctors. Sadly, however, Catherine did develop the disease.

Many years later, in the early months of the year, 2008, I had a waking dream in a strange house in Boston, in America, where I was to spend the semester as visiting scholar in Boston College, giving classes in the writing of poetry. It was winter when I arrived, Priscilla Street, in the suburb of Chestnut Hill. Snow was falling thick and fast. I was to stay in a fine old house, some ten minutes walk from Boston College and the Burns Library where I was to teach poetry. I was alone in a strange house, in a strange city, in a strange world. I had been listening, that evening, to the 'German Requiem', by Johannes Brahms, and the music was still sounding in my head. I had come such a long, long way. I find that by writing a poem about the rich experiences, the 'epiphanies' in my life, I can express myself better, tell the story in a truer way, and learn the more from the experience.

*Snow Falling on Chestnut Hill*
   *Denn alles Fleisch es ist wie Gras …* (Brahms)

It is late now in the day; that curving lane
with grass and plantain, clovers and pimpernels
forming a hump along the centre, seems
to be straightening towards a conclusion. I have arrived

in a strange city, evening; (I am hearing
Brahms, the German Requiem, *Selig sind …* blessed
are they who mourn.)
Boston. A big house, and daunting.

They have warned me of arctic chill
reaching this way, over Canada, the lakes, Chicago;
*Herr, lehre doch mich …* I have heard already
oboe-moans through the eldering house, thin

reed-sounds through unseen interstices: O Lord
make me aware of my last end.
The hollow spaces of the house
are stirred along their dust: All flesh, the music tells,

is grass. I listened, dozing gently, silence
encompassing, engaging me;
at the front door I heard …
(no matter, it is no matter). I stood

watching first snowflakes
visible against the street-lamps; there was the feel
as of the breathing on my face of a lover, as of the brush
of a kiss, sheer

arctic salt, a hosting. *Wir haben hier*
*keine bleibene Statt ...*
All flesh
is snow. And snow

does not abide. *Selig sind die Toten*, blessed
are the dead; they are at rest
in the Lord's hands. I slept
fitfully; strange

land, strange house, strange dreams; time
raddling me. I could hear
the sound of the deepest night
lying still under a delicate coming down of snow.

*

I have been wondering
about our blizzards of pain and agony – lupus, for instance,
immune systems down and civil war along the blood.
Prance of the alpha wolf. Bone

scaffolding showing through.
I lay, restless; my temporary home
whispered to itself in house-language, its wooden shifts
of consonants, its groaning vowels, when there came (Christ!)

a sudden rapping
against the door. I listened. Again,
rapping, urgent. I crept down. Opened,
I had to, street door, screen-door. Saw

darkness active out there, snow
swirling, a shape that
formed and faded out of the skirl of white and grey …
And she came, breathless,

shaking snow from her hair and face, stomping her feet,
stood in the non-light of the hallway and snow
pooled about her shoes. She, dressed in white,
reached to drop – 'a gift', she said – one

bright Christmas rose, helleborus,
white-petalled, dark-green-leaved,
across the hallstand.
'You!' I whispered. 'You?'

She smiled.
'But we laid you down decades ago,' I said, 'to rest.'
'Isn't it good,' she said,
'to hear the crunch, under your feet, of fresh snow?'

'You are … in body, then?' 'Soul
and body, body and soul. No longer flawed.
I passed where snow is a swarm of whitest butterflies
though I had been growing old with the wolves.'

'And why? Why now? And how …?'
'I bring,' she answered, 'gifts. Wolves, too, wolves'
she whispered, 'wolves are the lambs of God.'
'Our child,' I tried, 'is wrapped up tight in pain, God's ways …'

(I saw, then, the wolf pack, *canis lupus*, settling under trees, they
lie easy in the snow, you can hear their howl-songs, clarinet-calls
off-key in the moon-enlightened night, drawn-out off-melodies,
lauds chanted to the blood, their green-lit white-shaded eyes
sweeping across the heavens; *canis lupus*, grey-grizzled ancients
of days, the black, the white, the gorgeous fur and in the distance
I heard the freight-train howl of human hungers, a tailed-off

threatening horn-call across the night; wolf-pelt, winter-pelt, the
scars, the tissues, and always snow falling down the everyvein
of air)


'Be peacefilled now,' she said, softly as a brushing-by of snow,
'it is late, my traveller, live at peace in the rush
of arctic wind. We are all
sunlight, dimmed, all snowfall, thawed.'

'Our child …'
But she was already moving towards the door, her head
shaking; 'All flesh is snow,
snow-fox, snow-pelt. I have been, with you,

a lover, singing against the moon,
a lamb …' The door … I felt the touch of pre-dawn frost,
heard snow in its soft slide, its fistfuls from the trees,
'Wolves, too,' she said, 'wolves

are the lambs of God.'
'Wait!' I called, and reached
for her. But she was gone,
suddenly, and there was nothing, 'I have

questions … prayers …'
Silence, only, and absence. I heard still
the breathing of the snow, a car somewhere
climbing a hill. I stood in darkness. Stood. Perplexed,

as always. A snow-plough passed, the steel blades
scraping against the roads. Soon
cars, roof-racked with snow, would shift
like herds of caribou

down the long parkway. The first
faint light of a new day
touched the window. I saw,
on the hallstand, fresh and beautiful,

one hellebore, one Christmas rose.
I closed my eyes against the dawn and heard
Brahms again: *Wie lieblich sind die Wohnungen* ...
how beautiful your dwellings, Lord, how beautiful.

*Five*

*Poetry Ireland*

⤳

My scaffolding of belief, of Roman Catholic faith, and hope, was precarious at this stage. My sense of a loving God was shattered. I would have to abandon this faith, or live with it and find a more stable, more soundly-based reason for hope. Now I was in a cottage in Mornington, in County Meath, along by the estuary of the river Boyne. I had no job. I had two children, Laura, born 1975, and Catherine, born 1979. I did not want to have to hand over the two young girls, to be brought up by relatives, or even to be with someone else while I went off to work. The solution was to try and get sufficient income from reading my poems in schools under the Arts Council scheme, 'Writers in Schools'. It worked fairly well. And along with some radio work, some reviewing, I was making just about sufficient to get us by. And we had some good times: I had a blue Toyota Liteace Van; I had two mattresses in the back. I had a 'baby chair' fixed in the front between the driver's seat and the passenger seat, so we all three wandered off about the country, to schools here and there. The expenses I was given for staying over in a guest house or hotel we saved by sleeping in the van. I succeeded reasonably well with the camper gas equipment I had bought and so we three vagrants had many picnics and some small adventures. Life was not easy. But we were in a lovely place, we enjoyed the house, the two girls went to the local school in Mornington, hard by the marshes of the Boyne estuary. We got by.

*The Lesson*

The estuary mud-flats lie in drifts
and dunes; you would expect the Bedouin
to appear beyond the wadis, hear the thin

complaining of their goats. But long before dawn
the tide was full, smoothing gulleys,
salting scrub. The mud, dull brown,

is nauseous, exposed to the sudden savageries
of birds. The morning bus has ferried away
your child to her first day's schooling; she carried

a weight that will bend her back. You will
remember her chattering, a lunchbox, the gay
thongs of her sandals, coins for the journey.

Soon, along the estuary, the tide will fill.

Some years earlier, when I first grew aware of the fact that poets were actually living beings and that some of them appeared – 'in the flesh' – now and then to read their poems to a living audience, I was bemused and keen to find out more. I discovered that many of these events were held in pubs, where the till continued to bang metallically even in the midst of a poem being read, that the poet was present under a certain reluctant tolerance, that he or she was paid for reciting the work, if lucky, by a pint or two of plain porter, and that the audience, over in a corner, might chat away during part or all of the performance.

Being used to the professionalism of Cecil Sheridan and of show-people in general, I found this bizarre, insulting, irritating and in many ways a sorry escapade. Was there no such thing as a poet who might make a living from writing such wonderful work? I later attended a reading by Seamus Heaney in the poetry centre in London and was instantly struck by what was happening there. Here was a building devoted to poetry, with a poetry bookshop and library, an attendant café, a room for reading and a room for readings, without tills clashing and people muttering. How obvious the need for such a centre in Ireland!

It was the late John Heath-Stubbs, then almost wholly blind, who challenged me to begin such a thing in Dublin. I was in the London flat of the late Robert Greacen, in Pembridge Crescent, with whom I had begun a friendship and there were other poets present. Indeed this was a poetry society in miniature, the 'Pembridge Poets', a small group who met to read and discuss their poems. I mentioned how poetry readings happened in Dublin. Start a poetry society, John Heath-Stubbs muttered, find a disused building down the docks, get money from the government, Ireland is a rich hive for poetry, go ahead and set it up. It was then early 1978. Why not write to the newspapers and see if there was anybody out there who might be interested.

Innocently, as a simple query, I wrote a letter to *The Irish Times* suggesting that somebody should establish a poetry centre for Dublin. It aroused some interest and it was also instantly assumed that what I had suggested someone start, was something I myself should set about. Several poets wrote to me directly; some even offered money to get it going. Staggering and reeling and doubtful, 'Poetry Ireland' came into existence.

By late September 1978, the Arts Council had come in, somewhat tentatively, on the idea. I had gathered 'members' who paid a contribution and received a newsletter and a hand-printed, signed poem, in return. I had some forty members; I had some money. I contacted a few poets and suggested a reading … They agreed. I took the plunge. Poetry Ireland started with its 'inaugural' reading, in the Player Wills Theatre on the South Circular Road, on Friday, 22 September 1978. John Montague agreed to be 'president' and he read on that evening; I had a blank hardback copy in which I would hope to get signatures of the poets reading and John's name is first on the page; his comment: 'Glad to be here – and aware of the reasons for it – may we have good luck.' He was followed in the reading by the late and generous Kevin Faller, who signed, and wrote: 'Best wishes to John F. Deane.' The Gaelic side of things was represented by the most gracious and generous late Máirtín Ó Direáin; Derek Mahon read, and wrote 'that the work may prosper' and Paul Durcan read, commenting: '*Salut John F. Deane, toujours de l'audace.*' The reading was recorded for RTÉ by Seamus Heaney and a programme was later broadcast on the series Seamus was then working on, *Poems Plain*. We were launched on the high seas of poetry in Ireland. The rest is history, and a history that ought to be written one day.

I had been reading and enjoying poetry now for many years. I came to poetry comparatively late in my life. In secondary school I resisted it, as I had resisted so much of what they were pushing on me in that place. Even in university I found it, for a long time, merely a subject and I would have to get on top of it if I was to become a teacher. At length, it was Gerard Manley Hopkins who broke down my resistance and it was that great dragon set in the gate of his work, 'The Wreck of the Deutschland', that finally brought poetry into my heart and soul. And with that poem it began with the music of the language, for I simply did not understand what Hopkins was saying or doing in the poem. It was the great music of the words combined with a clear and wholehearted immersion in the beauty of the cosmos that won me:

> Into the snows she sweeps,
>> Hurling the haven behind,
>>> The Deutschland, on Sunday; and so the sky keeps,
>>> For the infinite air is unkind,
>> And the sea flint-flake, black-backed in the regular blow,
>> Sitting Eastnortheast, in cursed quarter, the wind;
>>> Wiry and white-fiery and whirlwind-swivellèd snow
> Spins to the widow-making unchilding unfathering deeps.

Because the music of the words and the movement of the rhythm touched me, and long threads of excitement ran up and down my spine, I spent hours and hours working through and over the poem until I had an intellectual grasp of what he was saying, coupled with a vision of how he was saying it. And I was stunned, it was a Saul into Paul moment for me and I know I had garnered great nourishment from the understanding and the feeling of the poem, and earned a stimulus to read more, and even see if I could try my own hand at poetry.

For years I read widely and indiscriminately, trying to make my way from the traditional old forms and themes of classical poetry up to the contemporary work that also touched me. Today I read with more discrimination, returning often to favourite poets that stir and inspire me towards my own work, whether it be in form, or content, or even in the imaginative leaps that push poetry onto higher levels. I come back often to the work of Seamus Heaney, Thomas Kinsella, Pádraig J. Daly, to Tomas Tranströmer, Denise Levertov, Jack Gilbert: refreshing myself on depth, breadth, music, imagination, form and content and voice.

And it took years, too many years, perhaps, to understand what I was trying to achieve in my own efforts at poetry, and how to go about it.

My efforts at writing my own poems began with 'theme': what had I to say, what would I use words for; and at first I could not find a theme, other than writing about my memories of Achill Island and its loveliness.

I was looking outwards at the world, seeking to find something in myself that I might impose, of relevance, or meaning, on that world. It took time to see that this was not the way to go.

As I read more and more contemporary poetry I grew somewhat scared of the linguistic pyrotechnics I saw in a great deal of such writing, missing any theme, not getting any sense of a *Weltanschauung*, a philosophy, a world view. Language for its own sake did not satisfy me. I began to seek out individual poets who did appear to offer some thematic nourishment, in poets like Herbert, Donne, Milton, Wordsworth … in fact I was rooting back into the tradition, growing aware that there was a 'voice', an individual consistency of form, theme and language that became recognisable after some time. Closer to home at last, I found such a voice in a poet about the same age as myself, Pádraig J. Daly, whose work I encountered in literary magazines. Taking all my courage in my hands, I contacted him and asked if I could meet with him. I found that he was a priest, an Augustinian, a poet whose sense of tone and form made a musical phrase that was satisfying, and whose thematic impulse was Christian, and Augustinian in the sense that he was impelled to praise God through an awareness of the worth of Creation. His poems were nourishing to me in my doubts and anxieties; they were contemporary, meaningful and I felt that if I could emulate some of his work, I would do well. The impulse towards working out my faith problems through the medium of poetry, began to take root in me, too.

I came into contact, then, with the poetry of Thomas Kinsella. Here I struggled with the work, taken to it, first of all, by poems that I had taught during my short career in secondary school. There was here a voice that was, I thought, cool, confident, classically elegant yet edged with a contemporary dissatisfaction with the acceptable and the easily defined. I found his poetry rigorous in language, pared and cautious in his lines, searching and honest in his view of things, engaged in actual living and suffering and searching for order without compromise. He was the first poet I encountered whose every new work appeared to move his designs forward another pace, whose commitment to understanding was never static, who gazed inwards in order to watch outward with greater awareness and perception. His work was, and remains, a constant in my reading, and a challenge to a purity of language and intent that is uniquely rewarding.

In an essay written in 1991, 'Some Affinities of Content', and applying her thoughts to 'engaged' and 'political' poetry (she had worked hard with the anti-Vietnam war groups and had even been arrested during public demonstrations), the poet Denise Levertov wrote: 'The tragic and fearful character of our times is not something from which we can detach ourselves; we are *in* it, as fish are in the sea, whether we speak about it in our poems or not.' In my own situation I was aware of turmoil in my inner life, of that 'deep spiritual longing' that was now hanging loose and unmoored. I began, though without being overtly aware that this was what I was doing, to apply what I was learning (through my own reading, and through the contacts I had made because of my work with Poetry Ireland, with some of the best contemporary poets), to my own struggle with faith. My longing was to work towards a voice of my own that would bring poems both objective and introspective, both personal and yet immersed in the larger whole of the actual world in which I lived, and to seek out the presence of real spirit within phenomena. The world of phenomena drew and draws me; I have been always vigilant towards the actual wonder of the earth and my physical surroundings. Ever since my birthing in the wild nature and loveliness of Achill Island, I have been constant in my ease and happiness amongst the fine things of creation. Perhaps I could rename Yahweh/Jehovah/ God, perhaps I could translate the Christ I had been trammelled with, into someone real and loving, perhaps I could see beyond the suffering to a world of ultimate love and caring. And perhaps I could not. But, I felt, through the imagination, through language, through poetry, I might try.

In the latter months of 1978 and in 1979, Poetry Ireland, in my care, presented public readings in such places as The United Arts Club in Dublin, the Peacock Theatre in Dublin, in Trinity College, Dublin, in the Cork–Kerry Tourist Centre, in the American Embassy in Dublin, and elsewhere: with poets such as Brendan Kennelly, Padraic Fiacc, John Heath-Stubbs, Paul Durcan, Eiléan Ní Chuillianáin, P. J. Kavanagh, Eavan Boland, Patrick Galvin, Robert Greacen, Monk Gibbon, Gavin Ewart, John Jordan, Paul Muldoon, Thomas Kinsella, Michael Longley, Dannie Abse, Somhairle MacGill-Eain (Sorley Maclean) and many others. Gradually we were able to offer readings to poets from further afield and it was through some of these invitations and readings that I came in contact with poets like Marin Sorescu of Romania, Alain Bosquet of France, Ivan V. Lalić of the then Yugoslavia, and Tomas Tranströmer of Sweden. And it was the poetry of the last of these, Tomas Tranströmer, that utterly changed my own approach to the writing of poetry.

I was born to a Roman Catholic family and culture in which everything in life was clear, established and unchangeable. Between here and eternal life there were simple, clear rules to be followed; outside those rules and regulations there was destruction. In other words, I was brought up to be impermeable to the things of this world, my focus was Heaven; the laws of Holy Church, impeccably observed, would bring me there. In tandem with such a focus, the poetry I read and studied, right up through my Bachelor of Arts degree in English, had forms and regulations that allowed the work to be called *Poetry* (capital P), as opposed to prose. Themes were pretty well established; the language was to be 'poetic', 'free verse' was still an abomination and rigorous classifications of theme and development were to be followed. I had not yet encountered any form of modernism; I had not been introduced to Eliot, or Hughes, or Kavanagh. I was impermeable to the magic of metaphor and contemporary idiom.

And then I discovered the poetry of Tomas Tranströmer, in a Penguin paperback, in translation by Robert Bly. Even the title stirred me to a place I had never been before: *Truth Barriers*. I read the poems through and, because I was still impermeable, a great deal of what was going on was lost to me. But I was shivering with the excitement of discovery and I knew there was something here I had to make clear to myself. I read and read again. The imagery was astonishing to me, astonishing in itself and in what it pointed towards.

> I read in books of glass but could only see the other:
> stains pushing their way through the wallpaper.
> These were the living dead
> wanting to have their portraits painted.

There was a sense of recognition growing in me, a contact with reality that suddenly opened out into realms of wonder and acknowledgement; I felt, for the first time, that I had broken through some 'truth barrier' myself. I had no Swedish, and yet I sensed that there was something lacking in the translations I had before me. I had become permeable, I believe now, yet there was a blockage somewhere, and I felt it was in the language and movement of the translator's work; something was not quite right, at least, not for me. I can only put that down to some sort of 'daimon' that spoke to me out of a hidden place in the work. A daimon that was calling to me from the originals. Thinking I had nothing to lose, I wrote to Tomas Tranströmer, care of Penguin in London, trying to outline what I felt.

The first certainty I gained that I had discovered a work, and a person, capable of answering my questions, not only about poetry, but about living, was when, eventually, and by what circuitous route I will never know, Tomas wrote me a long letter, saying that he was happy with Robert Bly's translations but that there was always, in translation, a culture and point of view out of which the translator works. And perhaps I, coming from Ireland, had a different emphasis, a different response to the poems. And he challenged me: why wouldn't I have a go, myself. I did. Tomas had enclosed a copy of *Sanningsbarriären*, published in 1978, which Bly had translated as *Truth Barriers*. Oh Lord! but hadn't I become permeable! Without a word of Swedish, or a knowledge of Swedish grammar, I set myself down to the task.

I spent hours in the National Library in Dublin, with the Bly translations, and the originals, and with a very fine Swedish / English dictionary. I felt, and this is the core of my belief in the process of translation of poems, that I had already translated the poetry of these poems in my own spirit: I knew the poetry, I did not yet know the words. On that basis, I sent preliminary translations of my own back to Tomas, directly this time, to his home in Västerås. I think I sent three poems to him and he sent them back to me, with approval, but with suggestions, clarifications, and (forgive me!) praise for my work.

One of the pieces was a prose poem, which Bly had translated: 'Start of a Late Autumn Novel'; Bly begins his translation as follows:

> The boat has the smell of oil, and something whirrs all the time like an obsessive thought. The spotlight is turned on. We are approaching the pier. I'm the only one who is to get off here. 'Would you like the gangplank?' No. I take a wobbly step right out into the night, and find myself standing on the pier, on the island.

Fine, very fine. But I felt this was not satisfactory for an Irish reader, at least not in terms of the fluidity of the movement and the magic of the language. I called it: 'Beginning of the Late Autumn Night Novel':

The ferry smells of oil and there is something rattling all the time, like an obsession. The floodlight is switched on. We are drawing near the jetty. I am the only one who is getting off here. 'D'you need the gangway?' No. I take a long, hesitant step out into the night and stand on the jetty, on the island.

Fine, too. But it left me a little closer to the inner spirit of the original, or so I believed. And there was another one: Bly had translated it as 'Street Crossing', and the first stanza is as follows:

> Cold wind hits my eyes, and two or three suns
> dance in the kaleidoscope of tears, as I cross
> this street I know so well,
> where the Greenland summer shines from snowpools.

Yes, lovely. I had a go at it, calling the poem 'The Crossing-Place', feeling that here we were dealing with more than a street crossing:

> Icy wind in my eyes and the sun's dance
> in the kaleidoscope of tears as I cross
> the street that has followed me for so long, the street
> where the Greenland-summer shines from pools.

Comparisons are odious! and what I intended, in my efforts, was to make the poetry more resonant to myself in English, to translate the original while first *knowing* the poem through and through. I am certain that each generation may well wish to re-translate poems to their own idiom and to respond to them in their own spirit; translation, after all, is a carrying over from one place, one idiom, to another. It was always my concern to carry over the poetry; I left it to the dictionary and to Tomas's generous and kindly pointing out of any grammatical or linguistic false notes I had played in the work, to set me straight where the work needed more exactitude. Eventually, all this correspondence and effort led me to publish the whole of that original little book, *Sanningsbarriären*, with Aquila Press in 1984. Because of what this work had done for me, I called my book *The Truth Barrier*. It was very well received and correspondence with Tomas continued.

In 1983 he sent me his new book, *Det Vilda Torget* and I got down to working on that in the same way. Tomas was so pleased with these translations that he agreed to come to Dublin, if I could publish the book here. In the summer of 1985, shortly after the birth of our daughter Mary (Yes, my life had come together again; I had met, loved and married; and more of this later on in this book.), The Dedalus Press published my translation in a fine hardback edition, *The Wild Marketplace*. Tomas came to Dublin and we launched the book, with the late and wonderfully generous Seamus Heaney giving the introduction and Tomas reading from the book. I was nervous that somebody might ask, (and rightly so, I thought), 'but Deane doesn't speak a word of Swedish!' I had my answer ready: No, not a word, but I know poetry, and I can translate Tranströmer's poetry! Nobody asked! I will always remember going upstairs with Ursula, with Tomas and Seamus, to see how our baby, Mary, was getting on in a bedroom in the hotel where we held the launch; both poets, later both of them Nobel laureates, leaned over the cot and pronounced that Ursula and I had done a good job!

I was more than delighted when, in August of that year, I had a letter from Robert Bly himself in which he says: 'I wanted to tell you how much I like your translation. Your words are active, lovely, vigorous, even impudent at times. That is just right.' He also asked me to send a copy of *The Wild Marketplace* to Robert Hass at Ecco Press who was preparing a selected poems of Tomas Tranströmer; eventually some six or seven of my translations appeared in that book. This I offer as proof of the huge generosity of spirit of Robert Bly, a spirit that chimes so well with that of Tomas Tranströmer himself.

Tragically, in 1990 Tomas suffered a severe stroke that has left him unable to speak, has caused paralysis of the right side of his body. Amazingly, he had written, in a long poem called 'Baltics', published in 1974, lines that foretold such a catastrophe.


Then, cerebral haemorrhage: paralysis on the right side with aphasia,
    can grasp only short phrases, says the wrong words.
Beyond the reach of eulogy or execration.
But the music's left, he goes on composing in his own style,
    for the rest of his days he becomes a medical sensation.

(in Robin Fulton's translation)

In August of 1999, Ursula and I were in Stockholm. We were invited, by Tomas and Monica, to come visit them on their island in the archipelago, Runmarö. We took a private ferry out there. It was a joy, and a grief, to live out the words of that first poem:

The ferry smells of oil and there is something rattling all the time, like an obsession. The floodlight is switched on. We are drawing near the jetty. I am the only one who is getting off here. 'D'you need the gangway?' No. I take a long, hesitant step out into the night and stand on the jetty, on the island.

We spent a joyous evening, even though Monica had to 'translate' what Tomas wished to say to us. Then Tomas played piano for us, wonderfully, with only the left hand. His spirits were high; his courage enormous, his patience exemplary. His winning of the Nobel Prize has been one of the great delights of my life, one of trust, at last, in the Nobel selection process. His poetry is one that opens the world to a loving scrutiny that changes the reader's view of things. His poetry broke so many barriers in my own life that any poems of worth I may have written, I owe to his original influence. His is a deeply human and resonating voice, capacious, exciting and immensely readable. And it is the openness of his imagination to the world, its actualities, its deeper resonances and meaning, that opened up my closed and doctrinaire imagination, to allow the world through the barriers I had set up in my early years. This is the very first poem of Tranströmer's that I read and translated:

*Prelude*

Waking up is a parachute drop out of dreams.
Free from smothering turbulence the traveller
sinks towards the green zone of morning.
Things flare up. He is aware – in the trembling skylark's
position – of the powerful system of tree-roots
and its curving underground lamps. But above the ground
the greenery – in tropical flood – stands, with
arms raised, listening
to the rhythm from the invisible pumping plant. And he

sinks towards the summer, lowered
through shafts of damp green ages
tremulous under the sun's turbine. Thus is checked
the vertical trip through the moment and the wings broaden
to an osprey's glide over the gushing water.
Bronze age horns
with their outlaw tune
hang over the void.

In the first hours of the day consciousness can grasp the world
the way the hand clasps a sun-warmed stone.
The traveller stands under the tree. Shall –
after the tumble down through death's vortex –
a great light unfurl over his head?

One of his preoccupations is with the difficulty, sometimes the impossibility, of communication. It's a subject often rehearsed in our era, but Tranströmer is at once more obsessive and less doctrinaire on the subject than some others. He does not move by dislocating grammar and language, but speaks of the difficulty in a poem that is uniquely straightforward:

*From March '79*

Tired of all who come with words, words but no language
I went to the snow-covered island.
The wild does not have words.
The unwritten pages spread themselves out in all directions!
I come across the marks of roe-deer's hooves in the snow.
Language but no words.

So, figures in a landscape; the difficulties of communication; the magic of metaphors; and there is the sense that life is truest in the honesty and integrity that can be found within the self, if that self can be got at. Perhaps, he seems to say, the figures in the landscape are too much taken with the things of the world, material existence that needs to be shed to find the self; a few lines from 'Postlude': 'I drag like a grapnel over the bottom of the world. / Everything that I don't need gets caught. / Tired indignation, burning resignation. / The Executioners gather stones, God is writing in the sand. A silent room. / The furniture stands ready for flight in the moonlight. / I go slowly into myself / through a forest of hollow suits of armour.'

## The Book of Love

Ursula. When I met her first, I said her name, Ursula, over and over. It was in Listowel, in County Kerry, and it was through a poetry workshop that we met. There was a quiet about the meeting that was yet shot through with an abundance of excitement. Both of us had known suffering and it was the suffering that had brought us to a state of acceptance, though filled with an openness towards life. It was a blessed meeting. We had touched, and had found love. We knew how to be still together, as figures upon a painted field. And as she was from near Drumshambo, in Leitrim, we shared a love and a togetherness in the presence of the natural world.

We married in June of 1984 and lived, for a while, in Sandymount, Dublin. We were near the strand. I walked, one day, the tide so far out it was a line drawn by a silver pencil on the horizon; the sky was grey, over the tide-pools and gullies, the ridges of the hard sand. I stood a while in the centre of a great bowl, on three sides the living city, on the fourth the sea; extraordinary lives delved and dug in the sand about me, black-back gulls were harsh against my intrusion. I had found love again and was amazed at my life's new energies, this rebirth, this redemption. I watched the spectacular dive of a tern, and a huge ship on the horizon shimmering in mirage; there was a far bass-organ fugue from the city's engines and a throb of life shivering again through my blood.

When, in May of 1985, a daughter, Mary, was born to us, then I felt as if the goodness of God had been made clear to me once again, the abundance of love and of caring, and a manifestation of a wisdom of which we humans have no true concept; 'for my thoughts are not your thoughts nor are my ways your ways,' as the Prophet Isaiah has the Lord say.

We set out to drive from Dublin, to Paris, where Catherine was to stay for some weeks with a family, to help her with her French. Ursula and Mary and I went on from Paris to Leipzig where Laura was studying German. The drive was a delight, weather pleasing, company great, the car behaving. Somewhere in Germany we stopped to spend the night; we found a bijou hotel, had a lovely meal, then strolled down to the river in the gathering dusk. The Moselle. Barges moved slowly by, no doubt preparing to dock somewhere for the night. It was warm; we were content. We paused for a while to watch how the fireflies, under the trees along the riverbank, zipped into their small flame-like existence, and zipped back into darkness. I wanted, then, to write a love poem that would be all about calm, peace, togetherness.

In the morning, we set out again, aiming to find the Autobahn that would bring us to Leipzig. We were on a smaller road and as we came round a corner we saw a rabbit; it was in terrible distress, having been run over by a car, we suspected, just in front of us, and left to die. We stopped, and put the poor creature out of its pain. Mary was so young, then, that she found herself unable to cope with the cries and suffering of the gentle creature and I felt that her tears were for all of us, we, dearly beloved, ageing into pain, and they were for herself, for what she had discovered about the world's loveliness, and the world's pain. And in that moment of new love, new joy, new awareness of pain, I felt that poetry should be able to touch, in some way, on the first day of existence, here where there is suffering and joy, evening, morning, and eternity.

*The Book of Love*

Perhaps the words of poems
I am writing for you now
may drift before your consciousness
(long after you and I are ghosts)
like something almost assuming
shape out of the long misting
of a long and misty day,
gone already but sustaining
among eternity's shiftless constellations:
that you and I have loved one another
across the in-between slow-motion times

we did not note exceptional, but were
the steadily sustaining everyday
alphabet of our togetherness.


There came a day, in Leitrim, when we were both outside, relishing the late spring weather. I had been watching bees among the foxglove thimbles when I looked up and saw the hawthorns, like Moses's bush in flames, but light with the fire of a radiance whiter than white. Iraq, Afghanistan, so many other places were again under siege and I was wholly conscious of wars, feeling graced and lucky to be in a place where weather appeared to be our major concern. I was then content in my love and life and, wishing to hold in verse something of the wonderful earth's outbreathing, I was working hard at my poetry. All around me were wonders of nature, birds, for instance, like the skittering sparrow, or the martins' flight, and wanting to honour along our roads and meadows the birds-foot-trefoil, the bitter vetch, the bladder campion, the 'crúibín cait', the 'heath pea' and the 'white bottle' (beautifully rich names for small and lovely plants not given pride of place in our living), I was imagining a Mass for all the dead and living who have been hurt by our culture of violence and untruth. As I stood and breathed in the blessedness of the world about me, I was rehearsing names and memories and sacred words, like trinity, hosanna, requiem, when all at once the colours, rhythms, music, the contained joy – all if it, converged to one softly moving presence, Ursula's, for she was then in her gardening stuff, working at a flower bed, and it converged, too, to one name, Ursula, and to one word, love, and I breathed out quietly into the world's breathing – may the God of mountain pastures grant you peace.


*Late October Evening*

We sat and watched the darkness close
– like a slow galleon under black sail
nearing; and grew conscious again of those
of our loved dead who might come, pale

in their murmuring group, up the long road
towards us. Thrush and blackbird hurled

valiant songs against the gloom as though
this was the first dying of the world.

You and I drew closer still
in the fire's glow, grateful this far
for love and friendship, while the low hill
melded with the dark and a perfect star

swung on its shoulder. When I turned back,
near sleep, to hold you, I could pray
our dead content again under black
sails, the tide brimming, then falling away.

In those years I travelled a great deal, to festivals, poetry readings, in
my own capacity as a poet and as Secretary General of the European
Academy of poetry. This academy was founded by the great French poet,
Alain Bosquet, in Luxembourg in the Spring of 1996. Its aim was to
promote poetry throughout Europe, an art form then suffering under the
stress in so many countries of economic development. I was one of the
thirty permanent members and I brought the academy to Dublin in 2001.
We presented readings and talks, and were, in a way, a travelling troupe
of poets, raising interest in the art. We also visited Lisbon, Genoa,
Helsinki, Malmö in Sweden, and other cities. It was an exciting venture
but one destined to fade away, as proper structures to fund and develop
the academy had not been created.

I also travelled, personally, to many other places. One of the more
distant places I travelled to was Trois Rivières, a city not far from Quebec
city. French was the main language there and I had to give a reading and
a workshop, in French, to a group of students. I found it difficult, very
difficult. On top of that I had arrived in Canada and my luggage had not
arrived with me; it took some five days before British Airways delivered
it to me. I kept asking myself, why on earth do I go on these journeys?
The answer was, of course, poetry, the presentation of my own work,
coming into contact with other poets, other ways of writing poetry and,
without doubt, the excitement of new and different places. But home
always called out to me; and love, and the fulfilled life I was now living
with Ursula and the children. And I spoke words in my mind, words that
brought me back home and close to all that I loved.

I hold to you, I spoke across the oceans, in the warm darkness beyond midnight. It is your presence that graces my days with purpose, and my nights with permanence. Sometimes I reach for you and there is no more than the down-current of abandonment, dreading your absence, wrapping me about. Now I have been sitting by a great river, willow leaves, green-gold, were idling on the water and for a while I grew attentive to the swirlings and inwash after the lumbering down-passage of a great ship, and became aware once more of the longings in me for perishable, lovely things. And you were there, I whispered, even in your absence. I remembered sitting with Ursula one afternoon, in Mornington, watching the ravaging, down-wheeling flight of the shell-duck, their wheeling and gathering, how they splash-skidded to a halt on the current's rush. And once we had sat at the lake's edge, and shared the gossip of our individual pasts, she resting her head on my shoulder, I holding her hand in both of mine, till we knew that day was an everlasting day, and we knew that the mystery of what stays forever is the mystery of the glory of perishable things.

*The Journey*

Should you then, at the threshold,
stumble and cry out, leaving behind you
the ones you love, should you have
bathed your face in the cold water
that brings you from the deep out into morning,
and should you then in the sky find tears –
flight dividing the waters from the waters,
the sea beneath you smooth as lawns –

you are learning again how you are froth
on the ocean, a bone-chip out of genesis,
how you are shiftful a while but urgent always
for the wafting of waters that will carry you
back at last to the same door,
the old threshold, the glad step upwards.

There is more to it, more to the rediscovery of love after loss, than the whimsy of body or of mind. I think of it in terms of the flight of joy that is the imagination based on real truth. So there is more to it than the quiet of a pitch-skin curragh upside-down on stones where wind and windlass and hawser rust-meld one to other at the pier's end. It comes close to being one with the great forces of creation. It approaches the heaving of the sea, even, at times the crashing of waves against the coast in dark-day Atlantic storms. It goes beyond the lift of the spirit that comes from great art, painting, poetry, music. More than the lilt of a Brandenburg concerto, or the shudder comes at the perfect conjunctions of language. It touches on the edge of faith in the transcendence to which humanity aspires. Near to prayer but passing beyond. A reminiscence. A profound expectancy. Something so great it judders always beyond reach, the way the ocean lifts in darkness past the strand-lights of the bay, past the mast-bells and the wine. More than the waters of all the oceans. The all of it. Then more.

My brother, Declan, priest, became seriously ill and I went to visit him. He was then in a small and lovely town in California, Pleasant Hill, and his cancer was terminal, we knew it. I spent a week with him and he was very weak. We talked a great deal, about Achill, about Mungret College, about his life in America, about San Quentin which was not far away and where he picketed whenever there was an execution scheduled. We talked, too, about family, our family in Achill, my family in Dublin. And we talked about faith, and hope, and Jesus. It was sad; it was disturbing, and it was rich and deep and inspirational. I sat alone in the front room one evening, Declan in his room upstairs, nobody around. I felt very much alone, until a beautiful moon rose slowly over the mountains. Just as I noticed that moon, I got a text message from Ursula at home, telling me she was missing me, and she mentioned the full moon that she had been watching. And I wrote, there and then, a poem:

*Blueberries*

I am in California. The moon –
colour of grandmother's Irish butter – is lifting

over the Mount Diablo hills and the sky
is tinged a ripening strawberry. You sleep

thousands of miles from me and I pray your dreams
are a tranquil sea. Eight hours back

you watched this moon, our love, our marriage-moon,
rise silently over our Dublin suburb, and you

phoned to tell me of it. I sit in stillness
though I am called where death is by; I am eating

night and grief in the sweet-bitter flesh
of blueberries, coating tongue and lips with juice

that this my kiss across unconscionable distances
touch to your lips with the fullness of our loving.


*Forever a Stranger and a Pilgrim: Denise Levertov*

When Denise Levertov came to give readings of her poetry in Dublin, for
Poetry Ireland and under my care, we got on together very well indeed.
She had come to some sense of the importance in her life of faith, only in
her sixties. I found in her, and in her work, a justification of my own
searching for faith through poetry, as opposed to the opposite notion of
using poetry to underline a particular faith.

   She came to faith, slowly, almost reluctantly.


   Tyrant God.
   Cruel God.
   Heartless God.

   God who permits
   the endless outrage we call
   History.

> Deaf God.
> Blind God.
> Idiot God.
>
> (Scapegoat god. Finally
> running out of accusations
> we deny Your existence.)

[from *The Stream and the Sapphire* © 1997 by Denise Levertov. Reprinted by permission of New Directions Publishing corp.]

Fighting with God may often be the beginning of a realisation that we do have a relationship with God. What we work on then is the under-standing of that relationship. Her absolute reliance on the imagination as instrument for poetry and for searching for 'truth', also bolstered my own belief in mystery and faith rather than what Denise called a 'crass rationalism'; poems, she held, must remain aware of 'the mystery of being'. This does not mean that poetry rejects ideas; in her essay, written in 1983 and called 'The Ideas in the Things', she wrote: 'The imagination does not reject its own sensory origins but illuminates them, and connects them with intellectual and intuitive experience.' Writing poetry is a question of composing the elements to a whole, not of imposing a whole on the elements. She was reading the New Testament, taking it in, transforming what she read – her encounter with the Christ – into imaginative understanding.

> Faith is rare, He must have been saying,
> prodigious, unique –
> one infinitesimal grain divided
> like loaves and fishes,
>
> *as if* from a mustard-seed
> a great shade-tree grew. That rare,
> that strange: the kingdom
>
>               a tree. The soul
> a bird. A great concourse of birds
> at home there, wings among yellow flowers.

The waiting
kingdom of faith, the seed
waiting to be sown.

[from *The Stream and the Sapphire* © 1997 by Denise Levertov. Reprinted by permission of New Directions Publishing corp.]

It was quite late in her life, after her political activism had eased, after her divorce from her husband, Mitchell (Mitch) Goodman, and when she had found some stability in her work in Stanford University, that she found the space and calm to examine what she knew was always there in her spirit, a sense of the transcendent. She is, as yet, hesitant and apologetic; in an essay written in 1990, 'Work that Enfaiths' she says: 'What a fraud I feel, sitting down to write about faith that works! ... I know only such faith at second or third hand: that's to say, I have just enough faith to believe it exists. To imagine it. And to feel a kind of pity for people who can't imagine it at all, who *don't* believe it exists, who diminish its possibility in their minds by calling it self-delusion or superstition.' During the years she was deeply involved in anti-war and other 'political' activities: marches, protests, etc., even spending some time in prison, she was criticised severely, even by her best friends, for compromising her poetry; this view she resisted, always. So when she began to see that her poetry might help her towards some kind of faith, she began to wonder whether this might also be seen as compromising her work.

'I have been engaging, then,' she writes, in an essay called 'A Poet's View', (1984) 'during the last few years, in my own version of the Pascalian wager, and finding that an avowal of Christian faith is not incompatible with my aesthetic nor with my political stance, since as an artist I was already in the service of the transcendent, and since Christian ethics (however betrayed in past and present history) upheld the same values I seek in a politics of racial and economic justice and nonviolence.' She finds that, rather than taking set views or religious tenets and examining them, poetry – the act of the imagination – can help find the answers to the great questions, or at least find the way towards the answers. She quotes Martin Buber: 'To produce is to draw forth, to invent is to find, to shape is to discover.'

In her poetry she sometimes took on herself the work and presence of other women who had come to a faith in Christ. Her poems on Julian of

Norwich are rich and deep. And she became 'the servant-girl at Emmaus', as she saw her in a painting by Velázquez:

> Those who had brought this stranger home to their table
> don't recognize yet with whom they sit.
> But she in the kitchen, absently touching
>
>                       the winejug she's to take in,
> a young Black servant intently listening,
>
> swings round and sees
> the light around him
> and is sure.

[from *Breathing the Water* © 1997 by Denise Levertov. Reprinted by permission of New Directions Publishing corp.]

I am often challenged as to why I should work towards a poetry of faith, alongside my work at other themes, and I do find the answer in the poems themselves, if they are of worth, for they show me what I deeply believe, after, and not before, they are written. Denise offers encouragement: 'This acknowledgement, and celebration, of mystery probably constitutes the most consistent theme of my poetry from its very beginnings. Because it is a matter of which I am conscious, it is possible, however imprecisely, to call it an intellectual position, but it is one which emphasises the incapacity of reason alone (much though I delight in elegant logic) to comprehend experience, and considers Imagination the chief of human faculties. It must therefore be by the exercise of that faculty that one moves towards faith, and possibly by its failure that one rejects it as delusion. Poems present their testimony as circumstantial evidences, not as closing argument. Where Wallace Stevens says, 'God and the imagination are one,' I would say that the imagination, which synergises intellect, emotion and instinct, is the perceptive organ through which it is possible, though not inevitable, to experience God.'

*Miscellany: Muir Woods, California*

⁓

How the best plans we make for a day out, carefully dividing time, measuring distances, booking lunch or an evening meal, or both, at special places, oh how these plans can go beautifully awry. And often work out much better than our human wit can ever anticipate. My brother, Declan, worked as a priest in the Oakland diocese of California. Ursula and I went out to visit him, in Pleasant Hill. He perked up. He told us of this great day he had planned for us all. A trip that would take us on a fine bypass of San Francisco, crossing the bay on the magnificent S-curling Richmond Bridge, cocking a snook at San Quentin as we passed, lunch booked on the great route 1, oh everything down to miles and minutes and even seconds. But of course, and against all expectations, the morning came wet and windy and within a few minutes of passing through the town of San Raphael, Declan admitted that he had taken a wrong road somewhere. An hour behind schedule we found our place for lunch, an old-fashioned British-style pub called The Pelican Inn. Crabcakes went down well before we headed back out into the rain. We had to skip the plan for a walk on Stinson Beach, north of San Francisco, the schedule already badly thrown into disarray. Easily enough we came upon one of the places Declan had planned for, the famous forest of giant redwoods, Muir Woods, California.

We could see that Declan was downcast, the rain had become a rather heavy mist and any panoramic views he had hoped for were now impossible. We parked among many other cars and walked a mucky path to pay our fee for entrance into the forest park. We three hesitated; after all, what pleasure would there be in wandering among giant redwood trees in the rain, what could be gained by that save, perhaps, an irritating cold? We drifted about for a while in the big souvenir shop, mugs and carvings and all sorts of touristy things on offer. We bumped into other hesitant visitors, we handled some of the stuff, we watched out the window, hoping for light.

Near the exit, just as I was about to call a halt to this dithering, we saw that the shop was offering for sale, at a mere two dollars a head, thin, lemon-yellow mackintoshes, with a lemon-yellow hood attached against the rain. We had come so far … Declan had had such high hopes … the trees waited for us. We made our decision, bought three macs and headed out along the signposted path. And entered a world of wonder and magic that I never will forget, a world strangely enhanced by the misty rain that kept falling, adding an air of mystery and enchantment to those high, magnificent trees. We walked, scarcely speaking, almost in a state of prayer, as if we moved through a vast Gothic cathedral, where all the columns were redwood trees, rising straight and true to impossible heights. And walked together for an hour and a half, stopping often to breathe deeply in admiration, to point out the wonders that we passed, to know ourselves human, to know ourselves small and almost irrelevant to a natural world of survival, and to an animal life that appeared to watch us with bemused attention.

Here were redwoods, *sequoia sempervirens*, steeple-tall, and we walked beneath and between them, awed to silence, through a past present to us in the trees that were, many of them several centuries old, the soft rain's sibilance holding all the woods in an embrace of stillness; we walked, side by side, and slowly down the rich aisles of pillared trees that soared, reaching high as old God's leaning, and we found ourselves insignificant, temporal beings, taken by the impulse to pray. For prayer can be wordless, the simple praise of our conscious wonder before the magnificence of creation where we move, reverential and respectful before a beauty far beyond our imaginings. And then we saw the owl, squat on a branch, watchful Methuselah, a barred owl, pale face, black rings about its eyes, mottled grey-brown head, the chest barred horizontally, the belly streaked in vertical bands; old hinge-head, this swivel-face and rain-owl, bemused at us who mooched by below, uncertain, turning to our cellphones for assurance, our cars waiting in the carpark, urgent for the forecourts, the switchbacks, the freeways. We felt that you could almost hear them, the redwoods, in the mists gossiping about the restlessness of humankind, who, for the moment, struggle with our illnesses, with the loveliness of the roe-deer skittering across our path, elegant and fearful, and the buck quick in his balletic leap into the ferns. As we turned for home, delighted and moved, proud of our achievements, we knew, in spite of our plans, that we had dipped our fingers in a sacred font and had emerged, fortified by sacrament, blessed again in spirit for our ongoing struggle with the flesh.

### The Reek

I had been speaking with Declan about our faith, and about the necessity of coming close to the person of Jesus Christ. I had spoken to him of my work, my efforts to write a meaningful poetry for our time. After I came back from California, there came to me, in a kind of dim light, the realisation of the need for our world and age to forge a poetry of personal encounter with Jesus. It irritates me that 'atheists' are basically encouraged to announce their atheism with a certain panache, but to be a 'Christian' writer, or to mention God or Jesus in a poem, draws some opprobrium. In a review of my poems, *Snow Falling on Chestnut Hill* (Carcanet 2012) in a literary journal *Ambit*, published in England, the reviewer begins: 'Can poetry of faith attract an atheistic reader, or is there an insuperable barrier?' She goes on: 'I can't, in fact, say why George Herbert's "The Collar" continues to move me in my latter-day faith-lessness, not to mention Hopkins' "Thou art indeed just, Lord, if I contend", and Donne's "Batter my heart, three-person'd God". Perhaps the finest poems defeat their origins. Despite these old favourites, I am now probably as biased against religious poetry as I may once have been towards it … I would never have read this collection had I not been charged with its review. That resistance would have been foolish. Deane is a true poet. There are poems here I would keep by me as watchwords, and some of these (not all) draw on faith-based language.' The admission ought to be a lesson to the reviewer and to all who approach poetry with jaundiced eyes (a kind of CCTV, closed circuit, mentality) because of the theme or emphasis. Indeed, I have often felt that poems by writers who are professed (proudly) atheists, often lack that imaginative freedom that faith offers; they miss, as Hopkins put it, 'the roll, the rise, the carol, the creation', and Denise Levertov's notion of the destructive power of 'crass rationalism' rings very true.

How was I to set about urging a contemporary quest, through poetry, for the personal Christ? Amongst my very early poems was the poem already quoted, 'Penance', based on the pilgrimage tradition to the mountain outside Westport, in Mayo, Croagh Patrick, the sacred mountain whose presence, just some thirty miles from our house in Achill, always loomed over me. I watched the people leave the island, many of them cycling, on their way to climb 'the Reek', to do penance, to salve their souls from the everyday. I only climbed the mountain when I was already sixty-seven years old, in September of 2011; this poem fused itself through my imagination, decades earlier.

But of course St Patrick, our national saint, was always close to my living, and close to my faith and heart. And the great poem, known as 'St Patrick's Breastplate,' or more poetically, 'The Deer's Cry', was part of my upbringing, my culture, my traditional prayer-base. I did a translation of it, to bring it closer to my heart, and published that in a collection of essays, titled *The Works of Love* (Columba Press, Dublin, 2010). St Patrick is said to have offered this prayer when he and some of his followers were being pursued by the king's men; they were all turned into deer and escaped, hence the title, 'The Deer's Cry'. In the poem the soul girds itself with the armour of Christ's presence to face into the day, a prayer suitable for beginnings, suitable for the start of any journey, suitable for the ongoing pursuit of that journey of life. It breathes awareness of how Christ cares for the soul on its journey, and how the battle the soul has to fight is rich with a sense of the great wonder and beauty of that world, a freshness and blessed presence that remains centred on Christ and fused to the beauty of all creation. It remains in the Irish consciousness as a morning prayer, as a prayer of protection, and we breathe it out with great pleasure. And it seems to me that it is rife with a personal awareness of the person of Jesus in the Trinity.

*The Deer's Cry*

I gather strength today
through invocation of the Trinity;
the Source and Sustenance of our being,
the Name and Nature of the Source
and the Breath that gives it being.

I gather strength today
through power of Christ's birth and baptism,
through power of His crucifixion and His burial,
through power of His resurrection and His ascension,
through power of His coming on the Final Day.

I gather to myself today
strength in the love of Cherubim,
strength in the obedience of angels
and in the service of archangels,
strength in the hope of resurrection,
in the prayers of patriarchs
and the foretelling of the prophets,
strength in apostles' preaching
and in confessors' faith,
strength in the innocence of virgins
and the actions of prudent men.

I gather strength today
through the great power of heaven,
light of the sun
and radiance of the moon,
strength in the lightning flash
and splendour of the fire,
in the swiftness of the winds
and in the depths of ocean,
stability of the earth
and steadfastness of rock.

I gather to myself today
the strength of God to guide me,
the power of God to uphold me,
wisdom of God to lead me,
the eye of God to watch for me,
ear of God to hear for me,
the word of God to speak for me,
hand of God to guard me,
God's way to stretch before me
and the shield of God to shelter;
the godly hosts to save me
out of the snares the devils set
and out of temptations of viciousness,
out of the clutches of those who wish me harm,
however far they be, however close,
singly, or in multitudes.

I call to myself today
God's strength against all evil,
against all cruel force and merciless
that may attack my body and my soul,
against incantation of false prophecy,
against the black laws of the heathen,
against the false laws of heresies,
against the lies and shams of idols,
against the spells of women, smiths and druids,
against those webs of knowledge that entrap the souls of men.

Oh Christ I pray protect me
against poisons, burnings, drownings,
and against all wounding powers
that I may reap abundant harvests of rewards.

Christ be with me, Christ before,
Christ behind and Christ within me,
Christ beneath and Christ above,
Christ on my right hand, Christ on my left,
Christ in my sleeping, and in my rising,
Christ in the courtyard, Christ at the wheel,
Christ in the heart of everyone who thinks of me,
Christ in the mouth of all who speak of me,
Christ in the eye of all who see me,
Christ in the ear of all who hear me.

I gather strength today
through invocation of the Trinity;
the Source and Sustenance of our being,
the Name and Nature of the Source
and the Breath that gives it being.

I came to Westport in September of 2011, determined to climb, at last, Croagh Patrick. At the base of the mountain, I collected a stout ash stick; I would need all the help I could get. I wore good climbing boots; warm clothing; a plastic mac against the possibilities of rain. I had a small back-pack, with water, biscuits, a bar of chocolate. I had prayer in my heart. I had a reasonable amount of determination. I had my mobile phone. In case of disaster. In case of success! There is nothing more actual than mountain.

There was sunshine. It was now mid-morning. I was Moses, gazing up towards Mount Sinai; I was a fallen angel watching towards Mount Hermon; I was the prophetess, Denise Levertov, looking towards Mount Rainier for her poetry. What I sought was Christ, to know him more closely than I had ever dared. 'Our fathers worshipped on this mountain', the Samaritan woman had said to Jesus; and here I was, hoping to labour in the footsteps of generations, as generations will labour on after me.

I quickly reach the statue of St Patrick that begins the 'stations'. The saint is standing, as I had always seen him stand in statues at the back of churches, as a mitred bishop, crozier in hand, in priestly garb, his right hand raised in blessing. He is a concrete presence here, whitewashed, too much the saint, for I would have him be the champion of the Irish people, a poet of Christ, impetuous in anger, gentle as a deer, indeed as that deer in flight through the woods. But I stood and prayed – in the name of the Source and Sustenance of our being, of the spoken Name and Nature of that Source and Sustenance, of the Spirit that gave that naming breath: As it was in the beginning, now is, and shall be forever, world without end. And I spoke the Name of Jesus to the soft air of the morning and listened, to the world about me, the distant ocean, the fields, the clouds, the sheep ... as if the voice of Christ were asking: Who do you say that I am?

The slope was steep and very broken; rivulets were coming down the loose-grit roughway, making me scramble, heave myself, slither, halt. I felt my bones were becoming numerable, sweat was pouring off me, and breathing was growing difficult. I sat often, gathering strength and determination. I had thought I might have found a poem somewhere along these unforgiving slopes, that I might rise on God's shoulder in a passion of delight, to whisper soulful prayers in his good ear. Now I knew that flesh, raw and thickened out with living, makes its own overwhelming demands. I heard, once, the child-wild scream of a kestrel, threatening and insistent, out somewhere over the slopes.

At last, with some relief, I reached the saddle of the mountain. Here the slopes levelled off; there was an easier walk along the ground before the next slope. I reached a rock and sat down, looking back on the wonder of the islands in Clew Bay. From where I sat, in late morning sunshine, the islands lay dark, like a herd of cattle browsing. It was a view to warm the heart, to kindle hope, to invite praise. And once again I thought of the three disciples, Peter, and James and John, the sons of Zebedee, and how they were taken up to the summit of Mount Tabor where Christ showed them, in the transfiguration, the glory hidden beneath his humanity. And Peter's fine and crazy suggestion, that they build up there the sacred tents of meeting, where they might remain forever. I turned now to look up the mountain and got a shock; the summit had disappeared, and just above the saddle, the mists were coming down, trailing across the mountainside like hordes of murmuring, grinning atheists. From where the slope moved upwards again there was now nothing to be seen. Below me I could still see the fields and meadows, the lower slopes of the mountain, all bathed in sunshine; the sea beyond, and the far-off hills, all were washed in the light of peace and visibility.

It must have been another hour and a half before I reached the summit. I was shivering with the wet, the cold and my own sweat. It had been a most difficult climb: the loose stones, the shale, the rocks towards the summit, all had been most demanding of a poor old, unfit gentleman like myself. The first thing to emerge from the mists was a hut of some sort; the ground levelled off. I could not see the chapel. I relaxed on the level earth and moved about, cautiously. The wind up here was very sharp and chill and I shivered, though I was still sweating profusely. When, at last, I saw the small chapel looming out of the mist, I found that it was shut. I seemed to be the only one about. I could see nothing beyond a few feet so the famed views from the summit of Croagh Patrick were not available to me. I leaned back against the shelter of the chapel and took out the nourishment that I had left, a bar of chocolate, water. I was already fearful of the descent, I was bone-weary and sore, but I was exalted that I had made it to the top. Amongst the summit mists I savoured the chocolate; I offered prayers, then, to my beloved dead and heard, suddenly, somewhere deep inside me, Christ's question put to me, personally: Who do you say that I am?

It was then that I made a decision. What was the purpose of my climb up here? It was, in a vague and unthought-out way, to come closer to the person of Jesus. I was now editing *Poetry Ireland Review*; what if I asked poetry to give me the answer to the question, *who do you say that I am?* What if I trusted poetry, that art and craft that had provided me with such understanding, strength, even income for so many years, what if I called on the poets that I knew to write some new poems, answering in a personal way, that question? After all, it had never been done, as far as I knew, this possibility of gathering together a new crop of poems on the person of Jesus. Was the world not seeking for answers? Was Jesus not the answer? I would do it. I would ask ...

But again, the doubts arose, the darkening and debilitating hesitations. What a foolish idea! these suggested to me. You will be laughed at; you will embarrass the poets; they will either tell you where to go or ignore your request, and then what will your relationship be to the world of contemporary poetry?

I was getting colder up there, leaning back against the whitewashed wall of the church, dreading the difficulty and length of the descent. I must move, and soon. And then came another strange whisper within me; what if I asked somebody wiser and with more wide acquaintance with the world of faith than I, what if there were somebody I could ask if this was foolishness, or a good idea? And there was somebody, the then Archbishop of Canterbury, Rowan Williams, with whom I already had a little acquaintance through poetry, a man I admired greatly, who was doing great work with the Church of England, whose profile on Christian topics was high. The playwright, Brian Friel, had sent me a book he had found, a book he thought I might relish, a book by Rowan Williams, *Grace and Necessity*, a book on art, literature and faith. I made a decision. I would write to Rowan Williams; I would put my idea to him, that I would ask as many poets as I thought I could reach, to write new work for me in response to the question, Who do you say that I am? and accept good work, either negative or positive, and put it together into a special issue of the *Poetry Ireland Review*. If he said, what a nonsensical idea! then I was clear ... If he was enthusiastic, then I would 'go for it'! I began down the mountain, still chilled, and anxious, but buoyed up by this decision. I would abide by the Archbishop's wisdom, if he replied to me at all. And I believed that something special had happened: I knew that the God who is hidden had drawn very near.

I began the descent, even more carefully, as it was more difficult, the danger of slipping and falling on the stones and scree, the wet and hard surface between rocks, all of this was obvious and demanding. Again I found the ash staff essential. I felt that some kind of promise had been delivered on, that I was working towards a newfound and uplifting faith in Christ, I found that I had come upon a further need that poetry might answer, and a trust in poetry as part of the ongoing project of creation. I came back down onto the saddle of the mountain. Again the world appeared bathed in sunshine, though the summit and its slopes were still lost in mist. I kept going, though my legs were paining me greatly and I was afraid they might give out under me! I had to stop even more frequently, but I made it! It was after five in the evening, and growing dark already, when I was back at the hotel. The bath I soaked in was one of the greatest of my life. The Guinness and the pub-dinner I had that evening were a banquet.

Late in 2010, my brother Declan's health deteriorated. He died in hospital on 12 December, and the next day I flew to California. The weather was bad; there were snowstorms, not only over Chicago where I changed planes, but Ireland, too, was experiencing heavy snowfalls. I already had worries about getting home. The plane was delayed on the runway for over two hours, in Chicago, so I arrived late in the evening in San Francisco airport. I hired a car, and drove to Pleasant Hill where I arrived, exhausted, well after midnight, at the presbytery where Declan had worked. His two great priest friends, Fr Brian Joyce and Fr Donie O'Connor, were waiting up for me and we chatted for another hour. For the next, difficult days, I was overwhelmed by the show of love for my brother that his parishioners (and his parishioners from his earlier parishes) displayed. The large church was crowded for the removal. The funeral Mass was attended by two bishops and an army of priests and there were so may people that the school hall next door was commandeered, and people were put in there, hearing the service on speakers. The people afterwards stunned me; so many of them queued up to tell me their stories of their love for my brother, how he had helped them, how they would miss him. One of them, a young woman, told me she was chaplain to the inmates on death row in the not-too-distant and notorious San Quentin, and that Declan had protested outside the prison every time someone was due for execution. In memory of Declan, the prisoners had spontaneously organised a prayer-service amongst themselves and a special service on the day of his funeral to coincide with the parish Mass. Tears of loss, and of pride and love, ran down her face. I was deeply moved by all of this, and very proud.

Rain was forecast, but the funeral day was one of extreme beauty, warmth and sunshine. Huge crowds lined the road to the cemetery, The Queen of Heaven Cemetery, where Declan Deane was laid to rest, under the hills of California, in a bright and lovely Elysian meadow. The next day the heavens opened and the rains fell all day.

I had heard, from Ursula at home in Dublin, that Ireland had almost shut down under the great sweeping in of snow. I had booked my flight home; I was worried. I flew from San Francisco to New York and as I approached the eastern coast of the USA I could see the ground below me white with snow. We landed at New York, and I moved as quickly as I could to the gate for Ireland. I had been told that Dublin airport was due to close, but our flight took off on time, and in hope. Grace followed me: our flight was the last one in to Dublin airport next morning; the airport closed because of the snow and frost. I got a taxi, 'I'm on my very last run already,' the taxi driver told me; 'we won't be able to operate; the roads will be closed.' I made it home, but had to walk, with my bags, the last stretch of the way, the snow being too deep for the taxi to make it through. But I was home, filled with gratitude, full of a faith that Declan had made sure that I would be home safely well in time for Christmas.


*Death of a Brother*
  *in memoriam Rev. Declan Deane, born Achill Island*
  *14 May 1942, died Pleasant Hill, California 12 December 2010*

Nunc, et in perpetuum, frater, ave atque vale

After the funeral Mass, concelebrating priests
filed out behind the casket, in white surplices
and black soutanes, like a fleet of small boats

leaving harbour under sail; they gathered
in late-morning sunshine to sing –
while dark-suited men lifted you carefully

into the hearse – the Latin hymn of our exile: *Salve
Regina*; male voices, a medieval chant, carried on the breeze
but all I saw was the dizzying flight of a hummingbird,

emerald with breast of scarlet, at the higher branches
of a tree, salutary, like an amen, like a reassurance
from the world; *vita, dulcedo, et spes nostra, salve* ...


    *


Brother. Belovèd. I have been following ...
On the way to school, remember, I
loitering; on the way home, scuffing
grasses by the roadside, or flinging stones

at high, unreachable gulls. Remember, evenings,
Bunnacurry, Achill Island, Co. Mayo,
how we stood together at the grove's edge,
stilled by the song of the blackbird, flute-rich

and visceral, *In the beginning* ... And follow still,
though I found you exhausted by that dread
and body-gnawing illness, and I felt shy of you,
we two, brothers, reaching out to one another

for comfort. In Pleasant Hill, breezes touch the leaves
into wind-song, while soul so clings to body
it is a passionate love affair, but will not last.
On the Golden Strand, remember? playmates

we built our moats and castles, learned to swim
in the easy waves of Blacksod Bay, stood
on jagged rocks at ocean's edge and watched out
over the vast uncertain, children, open, awed.


    *


We sat, again together, in your room,
the small gatherings of a lifetime, photos, books,
in an ordered disarray; and spoke of death, of faith ...

and you were famine-famished, broken; you spoke
the hymn you loved, your voice still firm
and I knew you had left me far behind,

struggling still, beloved brother, for reassurance:
*Abide with me, fast falls the eventide;*
*The darkness deepens, Lord with me abide;*

you tried the melody, but your voice broke:
*Change and decay in all around I see;*
*O Thou who changest not, abide with me.*

\*

God surrounds, the way the universe surrounds,
impels, as the universe impels – seasons,
fall and spring, cancer, volcano, song;
and there you were, too soon, almost prostrate

though I believe your Christ, eyes bright with gladness,
was visible to you, there, just out beyond
the Eucalyptus, your awkward, demanding, loved
Jesus, companion in the dread, the laughter.

Before Iliad and Odyssey, remember?
how big the meadows by the old house, how huge
the haycocks that we conquered, how powerful the weapons,
the wooden rake, the hayfork; speak to me now

how the world shrinks, how progress and neglect
make a wilderness, hiding the luscious honey-nests
of the distraught humble-bee, blotting out
two grinning boys, two innocents who stood

naked to the waist and red with sun. Evening
and I was walking with you round the parking lot,
Christ the King Parish, diocese of Oakland, California:
the cancer raddling you, slowing you to a soft-

shoe shuffle, you (this once) following, but the Christ, too,
walked with us, offering you the grace of suffering
while I stumbled, bewildered ever, incapable. Love
is a demanding fugue across our days, notes

of a rendered music building always
to a *Totenlieder*. You moved now, as Mary moved,
smitten by knowledge, setting out over the most
barren of landscapes, in expectation.

*

And here I am again, following, though most
unwilling. Schoolchildren line the road, the broad
Gregory Lane, Pleasant Hill, California, their hands
raised to you in blessing and farewell. Tears in the eyes

of many children. Tears in mine. The quiet hearse
moves slowly, sunlight gleaming on its chrome, its polished
mirroring black. I in the next car, following. Scent of eucalyptus
heavy on the air. You and I, Declan, children together, remember?

All of us children, *exules, filii Evae. Ad te clamamus ...*
I had rehearsed your dying, wondering at times
if this is dream or nightmare, everything coming apart
as cloud-wisps do, seen through the small window

of a plane, that fear when turbulence unsettles you,
and your fingers grip – in involuntary dread – the hard
seat-rests and you look for destination, the old
sense of belonging when you stride out boldly

towards arrival hall, reassured once more, on good ground.
And then we stood, sodden with our grieving, as you
went down, too young, out of the light, leaving us
to bear the unacceptable burden of your dying,

nothing between me and the dark, now you are gone.
And Brian Joyce, speaking the prayers out loud,
sending a sprinkling of water, like love-tears, towards you,
I dropped some red and golden roses down with you, tokens

of our incapacity with words. Perhaps ours is the dream
of blackbird, singing out of dusk, offering us all
the coming-together again, for the last time, of the light
and night. *Ad te clamamus, ad te clamamus.*

*Name and Nature: Who do you say that I am?*

The *Poetry Ireland Review*: Issue 112, Easter 2014: 'Name and Nature, Who do you say that I am?' It appeared, after a great deal of correspondence, enthusiasm and interest. Here are some of the initial responses to my request: Archbishop Rowan Williams: 'I was very much enthused by your project. Please be in touch about any help I can give with this – I'd be glad to support in any way possible.' Eventually he sent me a sequence of twenty-one short, haiku-style poems, one for each chapter of St John's Gospel. Fiona Sampson: 'A fascinating project ... and a fascinating, difficult thing to write. I can't wait to have a go ...' David Harsent: 'This is a fascinating proposal. There's definitely something for me in this.' John Burnside: 'Your message re the Jesus poem got something going again in my head.' 3 November 2011, Seamus Heaney wrote: 'I will definitely keep the project in mind. It's quite a commission, a test of truth and art, but one worth risking.' And on 22 November 2011, the late Dennis O'Driscoll wrote: 'Very many thanks for the welcome news of your *Name and Nature* anthology. I would absolutely love to contribute to it. From "Miracles" in my first collection to "Intercession" and "The Call" in my most recent book, I have been preoccupied with the issue of Christ in the world – a live issue for me.'

This is a tiny sample of the kind of generous and wholehearted responses that I got to my initial request for poems. The issue of *Poetry Ireland Review* eventually ended up with some fifty-five writers, among them four essays to serve as background and surround: from Fr Enda McDonagh, the novelist Colum McCann, Conor McDonough, and Abbott Mark Patrick Hederman. The Abbott accompanied his essay (on Rilke, and that poet's influence on Mark Patrick's vocation to the monastic life), with a copy of an icon held in Glenstal Abbey, Limerick; the issue also contains seven more icons, contemporary and beautiful, from the contemporary Russian iconographer, Valentina Aleksandrovna Zhogova.

I was, of course, working towards such poems too, but I did not feel I should publish anything in a journal of which I myself was the editor. But I studied, the New Testament and the Old, books on faith and on Jesus, and I tried to let my imagination work on what I felt and believed. It was towards the end of the editorial work I had done on this issue of the *Review*, that I began to write the series of fourteen-line poems that were to become the sequence, 'According to Lydia'.

## Give Dust a Tongue

I stood for a few minutes before the heavy old door of the parsonage. I was nervous, it was a visit I had dreamed of and prayed about, over many years. Now I was at the threshold, armed with much reading and many questions. The road was a narrow one and was, of course, untarred; a carriage had just gone by, drawn by two horses, and it had left a spattering of wet clay on the doorstep of the house. But the day itself was fine, though now it was early afternoon and I felt that soon it would be getting dark. Trees in the churchyard behind me were beginning to lose their leaves though the rooks were still bickering high in the branches. I took my fear in both my hands, drew a deep breath, grasped the great brass knocker and knocked, a little too loudly, I feared. There was a hollow, echoing sound from within, and I felt that I really wanted to turn and flee, back to the car, and away. But some grace held me. I closed my eyes, held my breath. Waited.

At last I heard a male voice calling; a door opened somewhere within and I heard light footsteps coming to the front door. There was a slightly fumbling, unlocking noise from within and the door creaked open. And at once he stood before me, taller than I had expected, thinner, his hair was grey, almost white, his beard the same. But his eyes, oh they were sharp, a greyish blue, piercing, though his face was gentle, welcoming. He was impeccably dressed, a jacket of – as it appeared to me – some dark worsted material, but adorned on the long lapels with fine geometric figures in filigree green, most becoming; this over a dark waistcoat that looked like silk; he wore breeches and silver-buckled shoes, a kind of white scarf, though it was not a scarf, about his neck, with cravat and two white tabs disappearing into the waistcoat. His hair was immaculately brushed and I stood before him, conscious of my own jeans and shirt, my badly-knotted tie, and my Guinness-branded woollen cap. We both stood, speechless, for a long moment, he looking me up and down with a wholly puzzled expression on his gentle face.

At last, I whipped off my woollen cap and, screwing it tightly in both hands, I began:


> Love bade me welcome, yet my soul drew back,
>> Guilty of dust and sin.
> But quick-ey'd Love, observing me grow slack
>> From my first entrance in,
> Drew nearer to me, sweetly questioning,
>> If I lack'd anything.
>
> A guest, I answer'd, worthy to be here.
>> Love said, You shall be he.
> I the unkind, ungrateful? Ah my dear …
>> I cannot look on Thee.
> Love took my hand and smiling did reply,
>> 'Who made the eyes but I?'


I stopped; he had raised his hand in a gesture that forbade me to go on. He looked utterly astonished. And, of course, this is what I had hoped for.

'How on earth …?' he began. But he went on: 'Truth, Lord, but I have marr'd them. Let my shame go where it doth deserve … Yes, yes, yes. But how do you know? Who are you? Where did you find the poesy?'

'Forgive me, please, forgive me. My name is John Deane, and I'm from Ireland. I've come to see if Mr George Herbert will receive me and ease my soul a little.'

'Are you a parishioner? No, no, no, how could you be. You say you're from Ireland?'

'Yes, I'm from Ireland. I have my car there, just beyond the church. I drove ...'

He peered around me, but could not see the car from where we stood. 'Carriage?' he asked. 'Coach, buggy, cabriolet ... And the horses?'

'No, sir, no. As you see, I am not of your time, nor even your century. I come from the ... well, I don't quite know how to say it. Anyway, I know your poems very well. I love them. And I love your Master, Jesus Christ. Though I don't know Him, I don't really know Him. And have come to ask you to help me discover and love him better. 'And know you not, said love, who bore the blame?' You see, though I am willing, I am at a loss, very much a frail creature. Love, Jesus, I need to know how to love Jesus better, person to person, I am a Christian.'

He looked at me, even more astonished. 'You are a ghost then? A spirit come to taunt me?'

'No, sir, no indeed. I am a spirit, perhaps, but I stand before you in the weight and dust of flesh, real, demanding flesh, body, limbs, all real, all alive. To you, perhaps, I am a ghost, just as you, dear Sir, are ghost to me. But here I am, after all, and here are you. You are Mr George Herbert, are you not? Parson of Bemerton and Fugglestone? I am here that you might help me, please, to know your and my Master, and to give this dust a tongue. And I know your words, Sir, and on them I trust: Love bade me welcome, though my soul drew back, guilty of dust and sin. See, sir, see, I draw back,' and I stepped backwards, a little, onto the muddy road.

Still with that look of astonishment on his face, he stood aside and said: 'Come in, John, do come in. This is an occasion, indeed, an occasion. Come in, come in.'

I stepped inside. It was a dim hallway, a door to the right was closed, one to the left was open; at the end of the hallway another door, and a stairway leading up from near that door. I guessed that down there was the kitchen and beyond that the garden leading the whole way down to the river, the Nadder. He closed the front door behind me and ushered me in to the room on the left. It was dim, too, though the window to the street was a large one, with a net curtain across the lower part of it. The room was neat, the furniture spare, strange to me, uncomfortable, but utilitarian. He sat in a leather armchair and motioned me to another. We gazed at each other for a while.

'I am a lover of your poetry, Sir,' I began, 'and it has helped me to a love of Jesus. But where I live, where I come from, Jesus has become more of a vague and mythic creature, losing himself among so many other figures of history. I need to know him better, to love him more, to touch upon his person with my person. I have come to probe behind the poems you have written, to be selfish and seek your help to lead me closer to Jesus.'

'I am a poor country parson, nothing more. What I have been, what I may be, is nothing compared to the love of Jesus. All else is vanity; all else is dust.'

He was silent a while, his eyes on the floor, and I could see some dream-lights flicker a moment behind his face. Then he looked up and smiled, weakly.

'You seem to know the mains; I am rector of Bemerton; I married Jane Danvers. I write my poesy for my own benefit, to help me understand. I do not know how you have discovered all of that, because the poesy is not published, nor will it be, though I hope to hand it over to my good friend Nicholas Ferrar and his Community at Little Gidding. That is a special place. He is a special man.'

'But,' I say, 'you keep reiterating that all is dust … Why then, did Jesus come amongst us?'

'Hah! John, it is simple: He who was the Son of God became the Son of Man so that man might become the Son of God. That is why our poor dust can attain to incorruptibility and immortality.'

He coughed, suddenly, and hid his face a moment in a fine cambric handkerchief.

'Forgive me. I'm not all that strong, you know. Or,' and he grinned, a trifle mischievously, 'as you are a ghost, perhaps you know that, too, and if you have come spirited from the future, you know more things than I can know.'

He seemed to reconsider his words and whispered, half to himself, half to me, 'A ghost, a spirit, come to me from who knows where, or how, or why? Is it so? Is it so, indeed? Perhaps I dream, perhaps I dote, perhaps I go mad.'

From where I sat, in his parlour, I could see through the window the side of the church adjoining the parsonage-house. I could see some of the gravestones, greening a little, leaning over a little, in the graveyard.

'Do you see Jesus as a social revolutionary?'

'My dear master Jesus, yes, but more than that, a great deal more.'

'He stood for justice, solidarity, peace, liberation?'

'Oh yes, all of that, all of that, and more. Those are great good things, but beyond all that is the proclamation of the Kingdom of God, a kingdom not ours to grasp, but freely given to us by God. The Master came to offer the kingdom to us. He proclaimed it. Men have died for it. The Martyrs, the blessed Martyrs sent up to God in flames, how we might envy their sacred ashes. But not all can be martyrs, I lost two of my brothers, you may know, Richard and William, they served England in the wars. Dust. And I knew King James. The good man had praised my oratory: dust! and I was friends with Francis Bacon and Bishop Lancelot Andrews. Great men of the world. Dust. But because of the Kingdom, in spite of dust, our faith still stands on firm ground.'

I had so many questions to ask him. This was a rare opportunity. Mr Herbert was sitting tall and straight now, in that high-backed, uncomfortable-looking chair. He gazed a little beyond me, reflectively all the while.

'Your Jesus …' I began again.

'Ah yes. The beloved. The Master. See, John, how all creation is active under the spirit of God, see how the trees in the garden keep the Master present with us, even beyond the boundaries of church. Treasure the real, the beautiful, the love. Beware the sleight of hand of the Romish Church. Man is God's image: but a poor man is Christ's stamp, to boot. All our fences and defences, all our arrays and our best days, our cunning bosom-sin, all of this the Master will bless quite away. Our hopes in Christ begin with milk and sweetnesses; with him there is no month but May; man's age is two hours' work, or three. Sorrows force their way in and Christ's strong hands mould our bones in pain; and so I cry, 'Dear God! though I am clean forgot, / Let me not love thee, if I love thee not!'

'Ah yes,' I chimed in with enthusiasm, 'a poem, a lovely poem, that. But may I say that in our time, I mean now, in my century, humankind, even the Church, struggles with the relevance and even the identity of Christ.'

'The Master incarnated to reconcile the world and God. The decision for faith must first be made. Faith is there, the sun is there, we bathe in sunshine, we live in Faith. Faith is not to be examined; it is. I have considered it and find it so. Remember, too, we must, mustn't we, that Jesus, my Master, lived and died for me; *pro me*, John, for me, the individual me that may be dust but this dust is loved since all His love and saving action were for me. Everybody can say that, Jesus died, they may say, for me.'

I paused to breathe this in. Mr Herbert was smiling at me, a radiant smile, and I was deeply moved.

'Bemerton,' I began, to calm my nerves. 'It's a small town. You moved here …'

'Yes, it's a small town. But a fine one. And ah, my dear friend, it was here I found, at last, my true King. Did I tell you, I was admired once by James, the King; here I have come to know a greater King by whom it is worthwhile to be admired. Yes, yes, here I am rector, of Bemerton, and of Fugglesworth. Here I have my greatest library, though in Cambridge, Trinity, I had books to fill a barn, here I have all I need, the most complete of libraries, the Holy Bible.'

I was surprised when the door opened, between the parlour and the kitchen, as I presumed, and a woman came in. I was again startled; I had expected Jane, Mrs Herbert, Jane Danvers, wife of the Parson, to be a dull and plain woman, of a later age than I now saw coming demurely enough towards her husband. I stood up, rather suddenly, and found myself embarrassed by the elegance and poise of the woman before me. I grew more conscious than before of my own clothes, their dullness, their indifferent worth.

'Hah,' George said, with a certain pride in his voice. 'Jane. Come in, come in. This is a visitor from Ireland, forgive his strange dress, he's from a future time.' And he laughed. Then seemed to hesitate, and wonder. 'You do see him there, don't you, dear?'

She gazed at me, and curtsied, smiling.

'Oh yes, George, I see a strange person before me. Welcome, sir, you are welcome.'

I began to reach out my hand, to shake hers, but withdrew it at once. She kept both her hands hidden in her broad sleeves. She stood straight again, gazing directly into my eyes. I was taken aback; she was tall and elegant, she was pretty, there was a very healthy glow on her face, she looked much younger than her pastor husband but what astonished me most of all was her hair; she had it held well back in some kind of wire mesh which in turn was beautified by the most delicate white lace, but the curls that escaped were of a rust colour, almost Irish, I thought, with an almost west of Ireland loveliness. Now she stood before me, and I was so taken aback by her form and grace that I forgot the courtesies, and remained standing and, if it can be said, standing in a sort of stuttering way.

Here, I thought, was a character indeed, worthy companion, helpmate, or even – and here I hesitated – head of house.

'I'm delighted and honoured,' I mumbled, 'to meet you, Mrs Herbert.'

'Oh dear sir, Jane is the name. Jane. And indeed, you are welcome. Please resume your seat. I will not interrupt. George, dear,' and she turned quickly from me. 'Here's Mrs Everett, Thomasin, you know, with her little boy Nathanael. Seems the boy has slipped off a high branch of an apple tree, and we won't ask, dear, what he was doing up there, now will we?' Jane turned to me a moment, and smiled, and that smile was a light in the dimness of the room. 'I am passing on to the garden, George; don't you think a tincture of camomile, comfrey and smallage should do the trick?'

George remained serious. He stood, with a little stiffness in his movements, and went slowly towards the small window at the back of the parlour and gazed out. He brushed, a little irritably, some invisible dust off his immaculate coat. 'I think the comfrey is rather short, Jane. Something else will do the trick, just as well, some shepherd's purse, or some knot-grass.'

He turned back and said, to me, 'Jane cares for the poor folks, you know, their bodies need just as much comforting as their souls. Bless them. My Master loves them all.'

He came back and sat down and Jane spoke again to me. This time I jumped up, and was amused at how she glanced at my shoes, my trousers, my tie, as if these things were very strange to her.

'You come from Salisbury?' she asked me.

'No Ma'am, Ireland.'

'Yes, yes, George said so. But this day, surely just from Salisbury?'

'I drove over from Ireland yesterday evening, from Dublin.'

She glanced at George.

'From Dublin? In Ireland? Drove? In a carriage?'

'I took the car, we have a Toyota Prius, a hybrid. The ferry from Rosslare, got in to Fishguard and from there drove to Bath. I stayed last night in Bath and drove up here this morning.'

She looked stunned. 'I don't understand, the horses? the carriages?'

I looked for help towards George. He was smiling.

'John is a kind of spirit, Jane dear, a benevolent one. He's from time future, if you will. He doesn't really exist, you know. He speaks a strange

English, too, and passes from place to place with the speed of an angel.'

She looked at me again, shrugged slightly, smiled, as if her dear husband had notions she could not share, and said, 'Yes, well, dear George, you know best. You know about these things. John,' she said to me, 'I wonder do spirits like you imbibe a little?'

She smiled at her own pleasantry.

'Well, yes, Ma'am. A little.'

'Good, and we have a fine little Salisbury Ale now, brought over this afternoon by poor Mrs Everett, part payment, you know. Would you like to try it? George does not indulge. Neither do I, so I don't want it to go to waste.'

I smiled at her as I relished the shushing and silken sounds of her passing out again towards the kitchen.

We could hear, faintly, voices from beyond the door. George seemed to fall into a study, but he coughed a little, and began again. 'How I would love if that which my soul doth feel sometimes, my soul might ever feel. But I am a crumb of dust. Times I fly with the angels and times I fall with dust. My Master's message is one of joy; he is God's definitive offer of grace, an offer extended to all human beings without exclusion. I am speaking, John, of love beyond measuring and here is the ultimate mystery, the revelation the Master brings is one of unrestricted love. Unrestricted. Unlimited. Love ...'

The door opened from the kitchen and Jane came in; she bore a small round tray, with a jug and two glass beakers. She smiled at me and set down the jug and one of the glasses on a small table before me. The other glass, filled with water, she brought to George and, as she handed it to him and he smiled up at her, she touched his cheek ever so gently with the tips of her fingers. She came back to me. I stood and she handed me the beaker.

'May I pour for you, John?' she said. I nodded. I was a little overcome by all of this. Before this very special woman I found myself shy and tongue-tied. 'Salisbury ale. It will be a great commendation for it if you like it, you a spirit, John. I will have Mrs Everett's heart all buoyed up. Take a sip, please do.'

She had almost filled the beaker. The ale looked a little smoky, a little dark, a little clouded. I took a sip as she watched me, a gentle smile on her lips. It was quite bitter and hard, but I could sense at once that it was strong. It was a thirst-quencher; perhaps a spirit-shaker, too. I smiled.

'It's quite wonderful, Mrs Herbert, thank you. I shall enjoy it.'

'I am pleased. Good day to you, John, have a safe journey home. Back to Dublin tonight?'

'No ma'am. I stay again in Bath. The Holiday Inn. Tomorrow I head back to Dublin. On the ferry.'

'The Holiday Inn? I don't know it. I hope it is comfortable.'

She was being polite. She moved away at once, turned back at the door, and smiled. She glanced quickly at George. Then she left.

'Dust,' I said again. 'You speak, in your poems, a great deal about dust. "Love bade me welcome but my soul drew back, guilty of dust and sin." Beautiful, but, guilty of dust?'

'What a wonderful word it is, John, it chimes and rhymes so perfectly. Just. Trust. Oh it was death calcined our hearts along with the Lord's to dust and ashes, so his life will turn our hearts to gold and make us just. Dust rhymes with lust and rust, too, but also rhymes with trust. We trust in him, in our Master, for the Kingdom of God, already deep within us, will bring our dust to gold. "When th'hair is sweet through pride or lust, the powder doth forget the dust." What fools we are, pomading and painting ourselves before the Lord. In the ultimate loneliness and complete darkness of his blind obedience, my Master himself willed to enter death, and all that he could do was to leave to the Father the manner of his resurrection. He rose again, and with that rising our dust was turned to gold. Ah my dear, dear Master, we must speak with him, we must pray, John, we must always pray. Prayer is the heart in pilgrimage, it is our power against th'Almighty, it is Heaven in our ordinary day, it is the land of spices, and something understood. Grace alone can open the soul's most subtle rooms. God's name is immortal Love, immortal Heart. And if we are dust, and we are, then how great the love of Jesus has to be, to listen to our prayers, to open our hearts to his love.'

It was thrilling to hear that strong voice, coming from a body that was frail and weak, and the faith and trust in the voice were compelling. In the blessed silence that followed those words, I heard the clop-clop-clop of a horse, and a carriage passed just outside the window. I glanced over and George noticed me.

'This ale,' I said, 'it's very good.' I had finished the first glass and was pouring another glass out of the jug. 'Gets rid of dust, you know. In the throat.' I tried to laugh, but the noise I brought out was a kind of splutter.

George gazed a while on me. 'You have no horse, I gather, to pull your carriage?'

I laughed. 'No, Mr Herbert, but we talk of horsepower; we judge the worth of the car by its horsepower. Mine is quite powerful, it's quite expensive, too.'

I found myself beginning, ever so slightly, to slur my words, and to be speaking of things he could know nothing about. I ought to take care. I might frighten away the moment.

'Drink not the third glass, John. The human spirit is weak, you know, very weak. Money is the band of bliss and the source of woe. A car. Horsepower, without a horse. Amazing. I am not sure I could manage in your future. It seems careless and foolish to me.'

George sighed and stirred a little uncomfortably in his chair. He coughed, drily, and I felt the coughing caused him some pain. He raised his hand to his lips. The room was dim. Soon, I knew, he would light the oil-lamp that stood on the table in the room.

It was then that he had a bad attack of coughing, so that he had to lean forward, place his head between his knees and the coughing was a racking bout, painful, dry, saddening. I almost rose to call Jane in, but I knew too much, I knew what this was about. Slowly, he quietened. I had left aside the half-empty glass of ale; I did not dare finish it, nor finish what was left in the jug. Gradually the attack eased and he sat back again, tired and weak and pale.

'I'm sorry, Mr Herbert,' I said. 'I am tiring you.'

'No, no, John. It's a pleasure, I'm sure. And these are the harbingers you know. And I am growing old, too, see, see the white, look at my head. My hair.' I knew he was not yet forty and still, because I knew, of course I was not surprised. 'I have a fear, though, a great fear. Not of passing out of this sad world, but of losing what I have left of mind; shall these harbingers take my brain from me, these sparkling notions; must I become a clod?'

I said nothing, though I was tempted to tell him he had no need to worry. He looked at me, a little slyly, though he smiled broadly. 'You, John, you know so much. You are from the future. I heard you, at the beginning, say a poem of mine. I have made a poesy, I have made several posies, as the days went by. But they are hidden away, as yet. And I shall leave them to my good friend Nicholas Ferrar, up there in Little Gidding, and it shall be his burden. But there are times, oh yes, I admit it, there are times when one wonders, one wonders. Ah yes, now you see the weakness in the pastor John, a little touch of selfish wonder ... But I dare not ask, I do not ask. But you may see how all of flesh is but dust, but dust and bones and sticks.'

He coughed again, but nothing like as bad as before. I stood up.

'I am most grateful to you, Mr Herbert, and to Mrs Herbert, for your love and care and hospitality. I shall leave you with a great sense of gratitude, so great I cannot rightly know how to say it. Your words, your integrity, your truth, your finger pointing always to Jesus ...'

'Enough, my friend, cease. I would talk always of my Master, with joy and willingness.' He got slowly to his feet. Then he knelt down, awkwardly, with some difficulty, and bowed his head over his hands. 'Come,' he said, 'let us pray together, just a word of thanks to our Master.' He looked up at me; I still stood. He shook his head, gently, and smiled. And said: 'John, kneeling ne'er spoiled silk stocking.'

So I knelt. And then I could not help it, I just spoke it out, not caring what he thought, how he wondered where I got the words from, how I knew the poem, how I cherished it.

> Prayer, the Church's banquet, Angels' age,
> God's breath in man returning to his birth,
> The soul in paraphrase, heart in pilgrimage,
> The Christian plummet sounding heaven and earth.
> Engine against th'Almighty, sinners' tower,
> Reversed thunder, Christ-side-piercing spear,
> The six-day world transposing in an hour,
> A kind of tune, which all things hear and fear;
> Softness and peace, and joy, and love, and bliss,
> Exalted Manna, gladness of the best,
> Heaven in ordinary, man well dressed,
> The milky way, the bird of Paradise,
> Church-bells beyond the stars heard, the soul's blood,
> The land of spices; something understood.

I finished. I had recited it slowly, with love and gratitude, because I meant it. He remained wholly quiet, and I knew he was taken aback, stunned indeed. George Herbert; poet, pastor, servant to his Master. We knelt there in utter silence for some time. Then he rose, awkwardly, and looked at me. And he began, and I knew why he had chosen these lines: 'Come away. Make no delay. Summon all the dust to rise, Till it stir, and rub the eyes; While this member jogs the other, Each one whisp'ring, *Live you brother?* Oh John, John, John, my heart, my spirit, my heart! Come away, Make this the day. Dust, alas, no music feels, But thy trumpet; then it kneels … Oh John, I can no more, my heart is full. I wish you well. I wish you safe passage home, to wherever you have to go, you with your carriage with the power of horses, but without any horses. May your Master be with you, forever at your side.'

My own heart was too full. I could say no more. I shook him by the hand. Then, daring to, took him carefully by the shoulders and hugged him. He almost responded, but drew back, slightly. So I turned and opened the parlour door, turned right in the little hallway and opened the heavy front door. Outside I stood a while, breathing deeply, elated and joyful. Away to the right, down the narrow lane, I saw a horseman come riding slowly towards me. The lane was spattered with mud. I crossed it quickly, before he could come and scatter dirt upon me. I went quickly round the front of Bemerton parish church. The Toyota Prius was parked where I had left it, against the old wall. I sat in, watched in the rear-view mirror till the horseman had gone by. Then I turned the car, heading west out of Bemerton, to seek the road for Bath.

*Hopkins: the cosmic Christ*

George Herbert's poetry continues to point beautifully to the truth that Jesus was a human being, wholly physical, man, and Son of God. There is the beginning of John's Gospel – after that great cosmic opening: 'In the beginning was the word, and the word was with God and the word was God,' comes the emphasis on the real humanity of the word: 'And the word was made flesh and dwelt amongst us.' The late and wonderful Sean Freyne wrote: 'The so-called "high Christology" of the opening statement which locates the origins of the Word "in the beginning" with God needs to be counterbalanced with the equally emphatic statement of the Word's true humanity, if the full significance of the Christian proclamation is to be appreciated.' It is clear that, as Freyne observes, 'It has been a perennial temptation for Christian faith to take one of these options, either implicitly or explicitly, throughout history.' To see

Hopkins's awareness of the cosmic Christ as in any way denying the humanity of Christ, is a misreading; if I take Herbert as pointing to the humanity of Jesus as well as to his cosmic presence, I like to read Hopkins, in some of his poems, as pointing to the cosmic Jesus, as well as to his humanity.

One of the most powerful, beautiful and relevant poems (in this context) written by Gerard Manley Hopkins, is 'God's Grandeur', written while he was studying to be a Jesuit, in St Beuno's seminary in the North of Wales, a place where he was most happy and where he wrote many of his very best poems, including 'The Wreck of the Deutschland'.

*God's Grandeur*

The world is charged with the grandeur of God.
    It will flame out, like shining from shook foil;
    It gathers to a greatness, like the ooze of oil
Crushed. Why do men then now not reck his rod?
Generations have trod, have trod, have trod;
    And all is seared with trade; bleared, smeared with toil
    And wears man's smudge and shares man's smell: the soil
Is bare now, nor can foot feel, being shod.

And for all this, nature is never spent;
    There lives the dearest freshness deep down things;
And though the last lights off the black West went
    Oh, morning, at the brown brink eastward, springs –
Because the Holy Ghost over the bent
    World broods with warm breast and with ah! bright wings.

That word 'charged' is itself charged with meaning; here, I find, it serves to suggest that God has given creation a charge, to praise its Creator; and it also suggests that the creation creates a charge, an electricity, that springs forth in praise of that Creator. In that part of North Wales, in the valley of the river Elwy, the landscape is lush and flush with beauty. It calls on humankind to lift up eyes and heart and learn how beautiful the Creator Himself must be. And that this beauty is there, visible to and available to humankind in spite of our best efforts to destroy it. At this time, the presence of the Christ was almost palpable to Hopkins, and his fervour and hope were almost boundless. He was young; a convert to Catholicism. In a fragment of an unfinished poem, this personal Christ was yet seen as one 'Who came from further than the stars' and 'Now comes as low beneath'. And for Hopkins this cosmic and this personal Christ was available in the Eucharist, where humanity can come as close as is possible to Christ the Lover in the breaking of bread, one of the reasons why Hopkins left the Church of England to enjoy the 'Real Presence', not as symbol, but as the thing itself.

And so, when I found the opportunity, I was deeply thrilled to take myself off to North Wales, to St Beuno's for a 'Hopkins Retreat' in the very seminary where Hopkins had been so happy and his work so fruitful. It was July 2012, and I was surprised at how quiet the ferry from Dublin to Holyhead was. Aware of the poem 'God's Grandeur', I relished the sight of gannets on the Irish Sea diving into the water from on high, and of other birds, shearwaters, skimming the surface. I was in search of Hopkins's Jesus and knew that Hopkins himself had crossed this part of the Irish Sea a few times, working for the last years of his life in Dublin, where he died, in 1884. As the ship came in to Holyhead there was a dense fog and the ship's great horn was sounding. I stood outside, watching the great bulk of this ship touch against the docks with the softest of gloves. The train journey across to Rhyl was an emerging out of that fog into bright sunshine and the seaside towns of North Wales. I spent that night in Rhyl, in a fine, small hotel right on the seafront, though this summer the 'amusements' along the seafront were almost deserted, sign, I thought, of humankind's great greed digging itself down into recession. Conscious that next day I was entering on a 'retreat', I relished a good meal in a restaurant with delicious rosé wine accompanying.

Slightly nervous about the coming days I woke a little early; the flopping sound of the flag, with its Welsh dragon, against the wall just outside my window, the squalling squabble-sounds of gulls in from the shore, the sudden alarming insistence of a police-car siren going by – these got me up quickly and determined to relish the silence and meditation ahead of me. I took a taxi out to St Beuno's and checked in. I was given a cottage just up the hill on the grounds; it was a very comfortable room, with an en suite. From outside the window I could gaze over a magnificent view of the valley of the Elwy; Hopkins would have gazed at it. But not far away there was a main road, with the continuous noise of traffic; Hopkins would not have heard that.

I had a cup of tea in the dining room, all the people attending the retreat were maintaining silence; it would take a little getting used to. That evening we began the retreat, with a talk on Hopkins. Oh yes, this would suit me very well. The retreat was being led by Fr Michael Kirwan, a Jesuit, appropriately enough. So our days began; Mass after breakfast, a time for peaceful prayer and meditation in the main chapel where Hopkins would have been, in some of the small meditation rooms where it is known he wrote some of his finest poems; several sessions of talks about Hopkins, and how his poems came from his studies of St Ignatius's work, the Spiritual Exercises and how the poetry relates to his, and our, spiritual life. I walked often in the grounds, and the weather remained fair and conducive to such walks. We were free, as adults, to take our own pace, our own decisions but I attended everything, trying to relate my beloved Hopkins and his poetry to Jesus, and to my own attempts to find that Jesus. It was all uplifting, moving and deeply rewarding.

On Monday the 23rd, there was a 'Travellers' Mass' in the chapel where I had the delight of reciting 'God's Grandeur' aloud. Late morning and I was on my way back to Rhyl, and then by train to Holyhead, and back to Dublin on the ferry. Enriched. Fully determined still to try and come person to person with Jesus Christ.

I found the cosmic Christ mostly in Hopkins's great poem, 'The Wreck of the Deutschland'. The Christ at work in this poem is an intimate presence and at the same time an overwhelming Cosmic presence. The poem was written, with permission, in the winter of 1875/76, in response to the death by drowning of five nuns and others, expelled from Germany by the Falck Laws. Hopkins wrote in a letter to R. W. Dixon: 'when in the winter of '75 the *Deutschland* was wrecked in the mouth of the Thames and five Franciscan nuns, exiles from Germany by the Falck Laws, aboard of her were drowned I was affected by the account and happening to say so to my rector he said that he wished someone would write a poem on the subject. On this hint I set to work and, though my hand was out at first, produced one ...'

This is the incredibly powerful opening of the poem:

> Thou mastering me
> God! giver of breath and bread;
> World's strand, sway of the sea;
> Lord of living and dead;

> Thou hast bound bones and veins in me, fastened me flesh,
> And after it almost unmade, what with dread,
> Thy doing: and dost thou touch me afresh?
> Over again I feel thy finger and find thee.

Here it is God – source and sustenance of the whole cosmos – who is invoked, creator, and sustainer of it all, and yet the stanza comes down to the closest possible personal touch: 'I feel thy finger and find thee.' There is awe in the poem, there is dread, there is the sense of the human being's, and the creation's, total dependence on God. The poem goes on to speak of the poet's terror before God, 'Thou heard'st me truer than tongue confess / Thy terror, O Christ, O God.' The response comes in the third stanza when, with a quick and determined gesture, the individual risks all and flings his heart before the heart of the Host. It is a yielding to the terror, to the power; the personal struggle with the great demands of the faith yields to the heart of Christ whose presence is so close. The poem returns to the cosmic:

> I kiss my hand
> To the stars, lovely-asunder
> Starlight, wafting him out of it; and
> Glow, glory in thunder;
> Kiss my hand to the dappled-with-damson west;
> Since, though he is under the world's splendour and wonder,
> His mystery must be instressed, stressed;
> For I greet him the days I meet him, and bless when I understand.

The poem is already moving into the realm of the personal response to the person of the Creator, proclaiming God's glory, praising the creation, admitting there are times when the human heart fails to grasp all of this. He tells how Christ's 'Pressure' and 'Stress' brings the grace of awareness into the soul, how Christ's birth, Passion, resurrection, touch the heart into accepting the mystery. The first part of this great poem, then, is a hymn to the 'anvil-ding' and 'fire' of personal suffering that brings the soul, along with the awareness of the wonder of creation, to the feet of Christ.

211

The second part of the poem tells, to this background, the story of the five Franciscan nuns and how the great danger they were in brought the leader of the nuns to the feet of Christ. A simple structure, then; general truth, followed by concrete example. Christ is the Lord of the seasons: 'Thy unchancelling poising palms ...' but humans feel they are immortal, 'But we dream we are rooted in earth – Dust!' an ending that brings us back to the heart of Herbert's poetry. The great scythe of death is part of the cosmic movement forward. The poem is more an ode, then, than a narrative though this second part shows how well Hopkins had mastered the art of narrative in verse. It is all subservient to the cry of the nun: 'O Christ, come quickly!' In part one of the poem, it is the self's encounter with the cosmic and the personal Christ; in part two, the emphasis shifts to the nun, and on to Hopkins's hopes for England and for the world. The movement is out from the self, and back; the heart in hiding faces the might, the majesty, the terror and – ultimately – the love of the Creator and the Saviour.

There is, in the later Hopkins, a deeply moving and sad encounter, and loss of faith in that encounter, with the Christ. In Dublin he suffered greatly, a physical illness that brought with it a deeply disturbing depression, moving towards despair.

> But ah, but O thou terrible, why wouldst thou rude on me
> Thy wring-world right foot rock? lay a lionlimb against me? scan
> With darksome devouring eyes my bruised bones? and fan,
>    O in turns of tempest, me heaped there; me frantic to avoid thee
>       and flee?

Now we are back in the beginning of the 'Wreck', when all is darkness and suffering, only now he does not 'feel thy finger and find thee'; the cosmic God has caused too great a suffering in the pathetic mortal man; some of these later poems are deeply troubling: 'Comforter, where, where is your comforting?' And in the darkest of the poems there is a sense that he has lost that personal contact with Christ which alone gives release to suffering:

> I wake and feel the fell of dark, not day.
> What hours, O what black hoürs we have spent
> This night! what sights you, heart, saw; ways you went!
> And more must, in yet longer light's delay.

With witness I speak this. But where I say
Hours I mean years, mean life. And my lament
Is cries countless, cries like dead letters sent
To dearest him that lives alas! away.

I am gall, I am heartburn. God's most deep decree
Bitter would have me taste: my taste was me;
Bones built in me, flesh filled, blood brimmed the curse.

Selfyeast of spirit a dull dough sours. I see
The lost are like this, and their scourge to be
As I am mine, their sweating selves; but worse.

In this poem, the 'bones built, the flesh filled, the blood brimmed' echoes, though in a deeply darker mood than in the 'Wreck', those earlier lines, 'Thou has bound bones and veins in me, fastened me flesh.' But it is his faith in Jesus Christ, in the Incarnation and above all in the resurrection, that eventually allows him back into some hope and trust: 'Enough! the Resurrection, A heart's clarion! Away grief's gasping, joyless days, dejection. Across my foundering deck' [and here we are back in the imagery of the 'Wreck' again] 'shone A beacon, an eternal beam ...

In a flash, at a trumpet crash
I am all at once what Christ is, since he was what I am, and
This Jack, joke, poor potsherd, patch, matchwood, immortal diamond
Is immortal diamond.'

So it is that both the cosmic and the personal, incarnational Jesus Christ, works his way through the poems of Gerard Manley Hopkins, offering a much more difficult though determined faith than that of George Herbert, and the final victory is achieved, in the poetry and in the poet.

During those precious days in St Beuno's, I came to realise a great deal more about Hopkins's view of life and of his faith. For him, and for us all, the greatest gift of Christ is the Incarnation, the taking on of human flesh and all the consequences of that 'kenosis', that emptying-out of self; 'It dates from day / Of his going in Galilee.' It was Hopkins's belief that it is mainly pain and suffering that open the heart to the love of Christ; when the heart is, as he writes, 'hard at bay', it turns to Christ for example and grace, that the heart comes to 'Hero of Calvary, Christ's feet'. I found moments in the rest-area of Hopkins's time that is now a beautifully restful chapel where I found it easiest to pray without words, sensing, though rarely enough, what Jesus had said, 'abide in me, that your joy may be complete'.

During my walks in the grounds and in around the local villages, I enjoyed even a shower of rain that made a slew of jackdaws in the trees moan and complain. I heard a chiff-chaff reiterate its chiff-chaff certainties from high in a dense oak. While I walked the corridors of St Beuno's, I was always conscious of the poet's steps, of his search for Christ, the broken, steadfast lover, the dead-and-gone, risen-and-ascended, and the everywhere and all-time Christ of love and generosity. An evening walk took me up at the back of the seminary, higher and higher through the woods; it was dusk, there was a cuckoo calling in the distance and I could hear the who-whoing of an owl somewhere in the woods. I stood a long time, breathing in the peace and beauty of God's grandeur, relishing a spectacular view out over the Vale of Clwyd. And one morning, as I wandered the grounds of the seminary, watching the beekeepers, men in their white smocks, their gloves, their veils, I relished the scent from all the flowers, wild and cultivated, that were thriving about the gardens. In a small hawthorn hedge I watched a wren, fidgeting, I would have called it, though I knew it was flitting, eye-quick, instanting, labouring in the great labours of their world, however small. A robin was watching me just as I watched the wren and there were larks filling the air above me with the richness of their watery music. One afternoon, I walked across meadows and through woods, up to the old Rock Chapel, startling a hen-pheasant into air; in the woodland there were wonderful blue and white and purple digitalis-like flowers, bluebells, and other wild flowers whose names I did not know.

I grew aware again of the wonder in the minutiae of God's creation, and marvelled how the magnificent and powerful God of the great cosmos, was also the gentle, generous and redolently artistic God of the little things. 'Glory be to God for dappled things – For skies of couple-colour as a brinded cow; For rose-moles all in stipple upon trout that swim; Fresh-firecoal chestnut-falls; finches' wings … He fathers-forth whose beauty is past change: Praise him.'

*Six*

*According to Lydia*

☙

Towards the end of 2013 I had all the material I needed for the *Poetry Ireland Review* special issue on Jesus, to be called 'Name and Nature: Who do you say that I am?' I felt now that it was time for me to see if I could answer that question more fully for myself, in poetry, of course. I had read and thought so much about all of this, I had received poems from poet-friends all over the world, my head was teeming with ideas. I had also been, with Ursula, in the Holy Land and savoured its spaces, its air, its landscapes, its people. But I needed, somehow, to distance a poem from myself in some way, while at the same time drawing what I felt from the deepest folds of my being. As sometimes happens, the answer is given as a gift, a gift partially earned by all the preparation that has gone before.

And it began with the distancing thought; I imagined myself as the woman at Jacob's well, the Samaritan woman and her encounter with Jesus; this has always appeared to me as a two-way encounter, both of the characters in the story studying each other, reaching for a relevant and meaningful relationship. How did that work? So, the first poem of this sequence began to take shape; it came out, roughly, at fifteen lines, a little messed-up. But to move on from there, the Samaritan woman was now out of the picture. But the distancing, placing myself in the shoes of a woman, that had worked well. Soon an imagined woman, whom I named Lydia, came to me; place her in contact with Jesus, see how she reacts. And then, quickly, the sequence took shape, and each piece worked out about the same length; so, naturally, a sonnet-type piece was the way to go. I began at the beginning; after that, the sequence almost wrote itself.

*Cock-Crow*

It was soon after dawn and he was out already,
raw and impatient, for we could hear his axe
splitting wood, the first dull dunts, then the quick
rupturing sound, echoing against the roosters' calls;
there was a strength and such assurance in the sound
the village came to itself with a morning confidence;
the thousand-year-old olive stumps resisted stanchly,
but he would later polish the wood to a perfection
smooth to the thumb. By noon he'd pause, listening
to the laughter of young girls busying themselves
among the olive trees; in the afternoon loafing-hours
he would slip away to some small wilderness
alone, as if the fruits of earth and toil were slight, a shadow
darkening the woman's face watching from the doorway:

❧

*Bedrock*

Wilderness. We heard first about locusts and wild
honey; then, demons and wild beasts. The absences, no
water. The sun so fiery that the low hills
shimmer like a mirage. There are cool, sheltering places,
occupied. Easy to believe in demons, so little sound
there the mind hums. By day the burning, by night
the crackle of frost; thudding stillness of the heart, admitting
wisdom, dust-awareness; immured in desert nothingness
and the struggle with the mind. Opening to loneliness,
to the holiness of the unresponding; garnering strength
against the worst that noon can do, or the trailing moon;
dying to flesh-hungers, earning a certainty
that washed him through with tenderness, that raked
spirit and flesh to wild uncompromising love:

*The Binding*

The lake's edge – generation after generation
depending, shallow at the shores, bronzewater, gold;
millennia of shells, patterned dull and gay, becoming grit –
profound, a harvest, what's left of innumerable deaths;
they have drawn the boats up onto the grass, and sit
examining the nets; the human heart, they know, is forged
out of such bindings, such husks, at the very lip
of wilderness. This day, out of a sky so bright
it chafes like silver, they hear the high-pitched cry
of a swooping sea-eagle ripping the air. The man –
in mulberry-coloured robe and leathern sandals – has passed
down along the margins towards the boats; at once
there is disturbance, a sharp kerfuffle at the lake's edge
and the brothers, without a backward glance, forsake the shore:

*Kfar Nahum*

Beyond the village, willows, scrub grass, small waves
frivolously fingering the shore; warm breeze under grey,
scarce shifting, clouds; the day lifeless, and everyday
ordinary; a fishing-boat drawn up onto stones,
no shore-birds visible; noon, as if the world had
paused, uncertain, waiting. In the crumbling synagogue
craftsmen and fishermen sat, bemused, the stranger
standing before them, reading, and expounding; as if he bore
quietness in his bones in spite of the earthed resonance
in his voice; the authority, the unaccountable wisdom
that had been concealed somewhere in the Torah scrolls,
the mourners, the merciful, the hungry. Puzzlement
among them, here and there a muttering anger. Words,
as ours, but new, and other. A man like us. Unlike. But like:

*Disturbances*

By sunset, in Kfar Nahum, he had drawn to himself
many of the broken, crazed and trodden-down,
the undesirables, the pariahs, the freaks;
the space between gate and lake was a market-field
of clamour, pleading, incredulity and tears. Soon
he was exhausted. A yellow moon
hoisted itself slowly above the village, and a crow,
lifting in dudgeon out of the roost, called a loud
craw! to the clouds. By now, we were unsure of it,
what had happened, for something difficult
was insinuating itself within the stepped-out limits
of our life, but we knew there would be consequences,
grave. It was owl-night, the bird calling out 'who? who?';
can what is broken be whole again, what's crooked straight:

*The Flowering*

That night we lit lamps everywhere, outside, within,
on grass and pathway, down to the shore; he sat on,
all light and shadow, his words gathering radiance
and darkness into their texture; we lived a while in an island
of being, apart, and unmanageable; and oh! the strangeness:
birdsong, cock-crow, bright-winged moths singeing themselves
against the flames; smoke from the oils sometimes
itched the eyes but we stayed, startled when he said: your
sins are forgiven! and no-one, there and then, doubted it –
we thought of our blessed YHWH; we thought of the stone
heads and torsos of gods in the city set on their shaky
pedestals, and the night swelled; as if the raw green stem
of the Pentateuch were about, latterly, to open into
a great red wound, like the high and blossoming amaryllis:

*Demons*

It takes a lifetime to cast demons out;
you struggle with them, you, demoniac, you, unclean,
they throw you down, you howl inside, you get
up again, you have to. Lest they destroy you. He
touched them, lepers, too, their sores, their bandages,
their dead eyes. He would take all burdens on himself.
Thirsted and hungered have we, for such as he, to enter
into the soul's holding. I have found, down in my heart,
there is a sphere so still, so silent and untouched
it is pure as the snow-topped summit of Hermon
glistening in the distance. He, gathering them all, to table,
the manic, the castaways, the hobbled (we thought him mad)
and there was laughter, and quiet and – I tell you this –
peace where never there was peace, nor laughter ever:

❧

*Table*

I need to tell of this, I need to set it down –
how he brought them in with him, and how they grinned
at the shaken host; servants, with disdain, offered water
for their hands and feet but the stranger knelt and
helped them: the beggars, the bedraggled, and the whores;
they reclined on cushions at the rich man's table: who did not
eject them, offering lamb and artichokes and goat's cheese,
wine and pickled fish and pastries soused in honey; they
asked for barley bread and barley beer. The stranger broke
and dipped the bread and passed it to them, told them jokes
and stories of lost sheep and prodigals and wheat seeds scattered
against the wind. It was, the host adjured, a ghostly meal, touched him
with joy and bitterness, this kingdom rife with casualties –
but it was I, he said, who found I was immured in poverty:

223

*Samaria*

Jacob's well, Shechem, route of nomads, revolt, crusade …
of people toiling down valleys of silence into exile: she
drawing near – heart torn by love-failures – to the source now,
the sustenance. The stranger, waiting; out of exodus and genesis
with demanding words. Between them, issues of time, of history,
the depths of the iced-over, petrified heart. 'I thirst': who, then,
is keeper of the soul in need: he, or she? Between them, between
past and future, the clarity of water in the moment of its giving,
words echoing beyond the sound of words, beyond clanging
of consonant, bird-call of vowel, how the heart, in its taut holding,
wants to yield, to the presence, the immediacy. She, later,
returning home, stumbles, her pitchers full. He
stays, on the ridge of stone, staring down into the deep
till the moon brightens, down there, in the uttermost darkness:

☙

*Papyrus*

(i)

The word, I have discovered, is food for my surviving,
this need to lay down words on strong papyrus, in strait
and patterned lines, hints of love and yearning, and now
this penchant towards sorrowing, for memory is uncertain,
inaccurate, and, like waters, fluid. Words of Yeshua
who sought to slip away, before dawn, to a desert place, to touch
his source and sustenance. For after all, after that mid hour,
life will not be what it was; what, then, happened? The word
*existence* seemed to shift, as boulders shift in a quake, the straight
line of living twisted back upon itself in a kind of anguish,
what we had accomplished suddenly became undone, the
comfortable dark was now backlit by a more aggressive fire –
for he had stood, tears on his cheeks, before the sealed tomb;
he called: and there was a death silence: I heard a hum

(ii)

of insects, somewhere the faint cry of a jackal, an echo
out of Lethe and in the heat of noon my body chilled:
slowly, they unsealed the tomb, stood at its gaping mouth
mute with darkness; the sisters clutched each other, terrified;
he emerged, slow, slow, shrouded in white cotton, like a great
woodcock with folded wings, body camouflaged in snow,
and it was I who called, out of a living hope within me,
*fly high! Lazarus, fly!* But he stood still: perplexed, perhaps
blinded by the sun, when the sisters moved to him, and the crowd
astounded, cried with a shrill ululation, like flocks of startled
shore-birds until he stood, freed, and moved towards Yeshua,
a lover stepping out in exaltation. I understood there is no such thing
as the ordinary world, that words themselves are not
transparent, and world became, just then, afraid of this man of men:

*Mediterranean*

Came that day on the beach; Yeshua stood a long while
and spoke, of love, of mercy, of tenderness; my spirit
sang. We grew hungry. And there he was, frying fish over stones,
with garlic, oil, fresh bread, and I could not figure
from where came all that food; there were sea winds, and each
morsel we ate spoke benevolence while the ocean, out behind us,
murmured its assent. He had his place now in my heart, no, it was
deeper than the heart; we had come for pleasure, what we took
was the scent of the sea, a sense of comfort mixed with dread,
the sunset pink of flamingos flying over. I remember the new port,
breakwaters, the Roman galleys, new economies; the stranger –
Yeshua – had taken spittle on his fingers and touched the eyes
of a blind man; but Yeshua had mentioned death and we saw,
beyond the grasses a small group, hostile, gathering:

*The Garden*

Dusk – the sun going down – threw long shadows across
the ground; he appeared, coming in from the valley, and collapsed
on the hard earth; somewhere a bird sang, though the word
'snickered' came to mind. I remembered Genesis: the Lord God
walking in the garden, time of the evening breezes. An hour
passed; the world darkened further; up in the city
lights flared. I thought I heard sobbing, even a scarcely
suppressed cry; he rose, and moved, stumblingly, back
towards the wall; I heard voices, protestations. Then he came
to fall again, scrambling on earth as if his bones were fire
and though I sensed rather than saw his body, he was distorted
like limbs of the olive trees. I heard weeping; I heard fingers
scrabbling against ground. Weakness, and failure; embarrassing.
Relief to see the flare of torches coming this way from the city:

⚮

*The Viewing*

When he was harried out to be jeered at,
blood-ugly, rag-scraggly, filthy with sores, I knew
he must be guilty and I was ashamed. He could
scarcely hold himself erect, they jostled him,
there was blood congealing on his face, his
fingers, even on his naked, blistering feet. He had no
hope, he was already stooped amongst the dead.
Like a fool he stayed silent, stubbornly so, though
words could not save him now. This was degradation
before the people, his agonies mocked, death
the ultimate humiliation, for even rats
will creep away to die, in private, in a dark
corner. We knew now that his name would be
forgotten, left with his corpse in merciful oblivion:

*Hill of Skulls*

(i)

I stood on the slope, at a distance from the other women;
it was done on the Hill of Skulls, dread place, to discourage
thought; high posts planted, waiting for the cross-
branches, the flower, and the fruit, where the dead earth
was rusted over with spilled blood; a little aside –
though within eye-shot – from the city's bustle and indifference;
Miryam, for it must be she, stood propped between strength
and failure, determined mother to the last. I had dreamed
he would put an end to violence. The big iron nails
were not the worst, though the heavy hammer-blows
shuddered the earth and shuddered my heart – it was the body
writhing in agony, chest strained beyond the possible at each
in-breath, out-breath, it was how humankind spits hatred
against its own, the tender-hearted, innocent, the children – but

(ii)

it's how things are, the soldier said, and will always be.
The moments passed, each one heavy as an hour; I tried
prayer, but to whom, or to what? The sky darkening, the groans
lengthening, the screams … He was burning. Near us the cackling
magpies. In the sky, the vultures. The way, he had said,
the truth, the life – is the way death, then? Life, the urgencies
only of the body? And truth, what is truth? His blood
mingling on the earth with blood of the contemned. Love
the final casualty. Clouds blackened; hot winds
blew in across the hill, shadows were dancing wildly
amongst confused noises. He cried out, though rarely. My
tears were silent, copious. I heard a distant, drawn-out
thunder. After such hours he screamed out, died; as if
he had exhaled, with his last breath, all the light and

(iii)

life of the world. It was all thunderstorms as they
took him down and as I hurried through the streets
people were staggering by, like ghosts. I never felt
so much alone. That was the most silent evening,
night was black and long and I armed myself about
with fires of spitting olive-wood; the laneways crawled
with furtive shapes; I clung, desperately, to the supposed
mercy of time; words had lost essence and would spill
like hot grease; how could the world know he had lived, how
could the word love be redefined? Everything unfinished, all
undone. But I had inks, formed out of soot and oil and tears
and would carve deep in the papyrus. I remember –
the mountainside – he said: those of singleness of heart
will be blessed, for it is they who will see God:

❧

*Sunrise*

So clear we had not seen it: in the giving away of your life
you find it. Soon after dawn I was leaning on the stone walls
of the vineyard out beyond the city; there was a well, timbers
covering it; I heard the wood rattling; there was a man
stooping over, reaching for a drink; he saw me, called out
something, waved, and was gone. Tricks of the light, I thought,
the sudden wing-claps of doves distracting. I stayed, fingers
worrying the clay between the stones. I had not even
waved back. Bright this early and I imagined the valley
singing softly. The intimacy of grape-flesh, I thought, the skin
peeled off, the dark wine waiting. The mind can find itself
so foolish, hoping for too much. The quickening of the heart
urgent against grief. Or urgent towards unspeakable
joy. And I stood there, baffled again by this one life:

*The Turning*

After the killing, there was no hope left, nowhere
to turn. We abandoned the city, wondering if we might
get somewhere. Sat, disconsolate, by the river, knowing
how goodness appears and is vanquished before it is
grasped. Wondering if there is a way for mortal beings
to start over. Someone, walking the same path, may offer
wisdom, and insight. Becomes, in the nonce, mediator
between place and non-place, life and not-life, death and
not-death. The day advancing, our steps more sprightly,
we would hold to light against the nightfall. Logs
blown to flames in the hearth; dried fish and olives, figs
and honeyed wine; the ready warmth of love, the torn hands
blessing and breaking bread. What the blood had known
now in spirit and for truth. And so we turned:

*Lydia*

I fear onslaughts of foolishness before the end,
the loss of wonder when the mind cools, the wine
ordinary, the bread bread. Do not fear, he said, only
believe. I work to keep the heart open, to hold to the blessing
that made me aware, then, I was blessed; glory in the once-fire
that will be ash, in reason beyond reason. I work to cherish
the variegated birdsong, the damson flowers blossoming
when they will. That I may ever overflow with Yeshua,
as a jug will overbrim with a wine both sweet and bitter;
for I know I will meet him again, the raw wounds of humanity
on his flesh. I remember the sea's edge, when, late evening,
he spoke from the fishing-boat anchored just off-shore: See
and hear as a child, he said, that the deaf hear and the blind
have their eyes opened, the lame walk and the dead rise again
and blessed is the one who does not lose faith in me.